# A Stranger's Eye

*A Foreign Correspondent's View of Britain*

FERGAL KEANE

VIKING

VIKING

Published by the Penguin Group
Penguin Books Ltd, 27 Wrights Lane, London w8 5tz, England
Penguin Putnam Inc., 375 Hudson Street, New York, New York 10014, USA
Penguin Books Australia Ltd, Ringwood, Victoria, Australia
Penguin Books Canada Ltd, 10 Alcorn Avenue, Toronto, Ontario, Canada m4v 3b2
Penguin Books (NZ) Ltd, Private Bag 102902, NSMC, Auckland, New Zealand

Penguin Books Ltd, Registered Offices: Harmondsworth, Middlesex, England

First published 2000
10 9 8 7 6 5 4 3 2 1

Extracts from 'A Retrospect' and 'The Ministry of Fear'
by Seamus Heaney appear by kind permission of Faber and Faber Ltd.

Set in 13.5/16 pt Monotype Bembo
Typeset by Rowland Phototypesetting Ltd, Bury St Edmunds, Suffolk
Printed in Great Britain by Clays Ltd, St Ives plc

A CIP catalogue record for this book is available from the British Library

ISBN 0-670-88839-7

# Contents

# Prologue
# A Land of Milk and Oranges

I was born in Britain, but it was not my country. My people came from the island next door. They arrived in 1960 with thousands of others who were sailing in the same direction for work. In Camden Town my parents found a flat among the other exiles and waited for the birth of their first child. They had arrived in a Britain ruled by the last true 'One Nation' Tory cabinet. The previous year Harold Macmillan had led the Conservatives to victory in the General Election with a comfortable majority of a hundred seats. Britain was in the midst of its retreat from empire – India was gone, Africa was going – but the country was stable and relatively prosperous; historians might later conclude that this was a period of stagnation in Britain, but to my mother in particular the new country was a place of shelter. She loved Britain. 'Imagine a place where they give mothers free milk and orange juice for their children,' she said, 'and free medicine and rent money too.'

I was about seven when she described the circumstances of my British birth. There was still a sense of wonder in her voice. The land of milk and oranges had been good to my mother. Penniless and left to her own devices by an alcoholic husband, she had given birth to her first child in the maternity ward of University College Hospital, St Pancras, London. A London taxi driver had noticed her slumped in a shop doorway and taken her gratis to hospital. There, as a guest of the welfare state, my mother brought me squealing into the world. She remembers sharing a ward with women from many different countries. What she liked was that nobody at the hospital made you feel second best. The care you were being given was your right, not a favour, she would later tell me. At home in Ireland in the 1950s, Catholic bishops had destroyed the government's plan to introduce a comprehensive health care scheme for mothers and their children. It was, they believed, a socialistic virus in a Catholic country. To my mother, down on her luck with a child about to be born, the munificence of the National Health Service was a remarkable deliverance. The idea that anyone could walk in off the streets and be taken care of!

Our Dublin neighbour Breda Thunder agreed. She lived next door to us in the big council estate where I spent my early childhood years. Breda had worked in a factory in Birmingham, where her aunt ran a boarding house for Irish labourers. 'Damn glad we were of England, I can tell ye,' she would proclaim. She had stronger reasons for gratitude. Her father had served with the British army in the First World War, a 'shilling a day' man who'd seen the Somme and gone into Russia in 1919. Half of Dublin would have starved without the wage money from the British army, she said. Her husband's family also had strong connections with the British forces. Upstairs in Breda's house there was a little wardrobe in which she kept the dress uniform belonging to her brother-in-law, Paddy Thunder. Paddy was killed in action with the Irish Guards in Aden. I remember as a child sneaking upstairs and opening the wardrobe, running my hands over the thick fabric of his uniform and then racing out of the room, terrified of the ghost of a dead British soldier. Paddy was buried in the British military cemetery in Silent Valley in what is now Yemen. He was killed in the sixties before the Troubles up North got started. Had be been still alive and serving in the British army after 1970, the threat from the IRA would have ended his visits home. To them he would have been a lackey of the Crown and a traitor to his people.

I would later conclude that the relationship with the big island next door was profoundly schizophrenic: on one hand the cause of all our ills, on the other our economic salvation. In the stagnant post-war years the Irish poor – urban and rural – took the mailboats to Holyhead and Liverpool in ever increasing numbers. There was a popular song at the time that briefly made an appearance in the charts: 'Many Young Men of Twenty Said Goodbye'. My uncle, who'd travelled from Kerry to Colchester in search of work, wrote the song. There was hardly a family in the country outside the small middle class who didn't experience the pain of enforced emigration. My family sought work in Britain, as did my wife's parents. She too was born in London, another child of a vast diaspora that huddled around the cities of London, Birmingham, Coventry, Manchester and Liverpool.

They worked on building sites, on the buses, in pubs. They listened to English comedians make Irish jokes and learned to grit their teeth; they worked and sent money home. A great many of them stayed on. Their children became British citizens, though they were rarely allowed to forget that they were Irish under the skin. In time they would be replaced in the tougher jobs by West Indians, Somalis, Eastern Europeans. Their children would go to British universities and become part of the burgeoning middle class. They assimilated, though their parents always kept one eye to home.

Without the safety valve of the British labour market, Ireland might well have experienced serious instability. Our politicians and Church leaders knew this but pretended otherwise. We all knew it. And Britain didn't just offer jobs; it was where we exported (and still do) the shame of tens of thousands of unwanted pregnancies. The National Health Service did what our own laws forbade, provided abortions to frightened young women while establishment Ireland looked the other way.

As a child I had a vaguely hostile attitude to the country of my birth. It wasn't transmitted by my parents, both of whom resisted any tendency towards atavism. But an undercurrent of hostility towards the British ran through our early education; I learned a lot about British atrocities in Ireland, but little else about the country that I can remember. The idea that part of the island I lived on was considered British by a majority of its occupants was something I never accepted. I'd been taught that the North was British in name only. Some fine day and they'd be sent packing. I knew nothing about the island next door, and in the absence of knowledge I was subject to the influence of the school-teachers and balladeers who defined much of the popular culture of the era. But it wasn't a genuinely antagonistic relationship, more a subdued national ritual that occasionally erupted into belligerent shouting across the water. The eruption of the Northern Troubles sharpened the atmosphere considerably; in the wake of Bloody Sunday, crowds burned the British Embassy in Dublin. I found myself veering between anger at Britain and a quiet shame at the atrocities being perpetrated by the IRA in the name of all Irishmen. Yet the truth is that all of that happened on the periphery of my life. Had I grown up on the Falls Road, it would have been very different. But as a child in a Southern city, I was largely untouched by the dramas unfolding in Belfast and Derry.

★

As the sixties progressed we were increasingly prone to the influence of contemporary British culture. The Beatles and the Rolling Stones were mobbed when they came to play Dublin; the comics we read – *The Victor, Hotspur, Hornet* – were filled with the heroic exploits of British soldiers fighting the Huns and Japs. I was taken to see the film *The Battle of Britain* and sat cheering with hundreds of other Dublin schoolboys as the RAF drove the Luftwaffe from the skies over Kent. And one memorable night at the end of the decade British television arrived. Suddenly we had *Blue Peter* and *Jackanory* and *Top of the Pops* and *Coronation Street*. The alien accents became part of our daily life; the cultural separation between my world and that of a child living in London or Manchester was increasingly blurred. We cheered for England in World Cup football (this was long before an Englishman, Jack Charlton, brought an Irish side to the competition) and the teams we supported were British. I was a Man United fan along with half the population of the country. English tabloid newspapers were also starting to enjoy widespread circulation in urban areas: my first memory of a newspaper front page is of walking into a neighbour's kitchen when I was about nine and seeing a copy of the *News of the World*. It carried a banner headline announcing that an actress named Sharon Tate had been brutally murdered in Los Angeles.

I visited Britain twice as a child. Of the first journey I have only the vaguest of memories. Late night on a train travelling down to London from the Welsh coast. A family sitting opposite us with children the same age. Their father spoke with an Irish accent but the kids were English. I remember being confused by that. How could you be Irish and English, I asked my mother. I don't remember her answer, but I do remember the names of stations – Crewe,

Rugby, Chester – crackling on the tannoy and the great noise of the city when we got off the train in London. I remember men with black faces, men with turbans, red buses and black taxis, and an Indian takeaway eaten on the floor of a guest house on Ebury Street. That was London in 1968. It was bigger and noisier than anywhere I'd ever been before and it frightened me.

I came again when I was a teenager, this time with a company from the Catholic Boy Scouts of Ireland. We were camping in Chingford in Essex, but we made for the West End of London whenever we could. I remember that there were Girl Guides from the north of England on the trip. They were the same age as us, but seemed light years more sophisticated. We kept our distance. On that trip I discovered pornography and French letters. The former I contemplated in nervous astonishment, the latter I had no use for, but still kept one in my pocket for months afterwards. On our way back to Ireland we hid magazines and condoms in our rucksacks. Both items were banned at home, and we sweated our way nervously past the customs officers in Cork Harbour. There were two short visits to Britain in my twenties, both to rugby matches at Twickenham, which passed in a blur of late nights and heavy drinking. In all, my first-hand knowledge of Britain came down to four quick visits. I had a jumbled understanding of our shared history, I cheered for Manchester United, and I read the *New Musical Express*.

I knew nothing. This was exactly the situation when I was given the job of Ireland Correspondent with the British Broadcasting Corporation. On my first day in the BBC, a subeditor in radio news came over and asked if I knew any Irish jokes. Bristling, I replied that we'd had seven hundred

years of them . . . they were called the English. The subeditor retreated with a red face. I was very pleased with myself
at the time, but the truth is that I overreacted. The subeditor
was a very rare creature. Nobody else seemed to care where
I came from; in fact they went out of their way to make me
feel that I belonged. If anything the English tended to defer
to me rather ludicrously on matters Irish; they seemed to
regard the Irish Troubles as one of the great mysteries of
history. You had to be Irish to make sense of it all. The fact
that it was a local variation on the theme of intolerance that
had bedevilled the world since creation escaped many of
my colleagues.

After a few weeks' acclimatization in London, the BBC
sent me back to Ireland to report the ongoing violence and
struggle for a political solution. These were years of drift in
Northern Ireland. The violence was killing between sixty
and a hundred people every year, and the politicians were
shouting and not hearing. Yet, beneath the surface, attitudes
were changing. Strands of moderation were emerging among
the previously recalcitrant Republican and Unionist blocs.
It would take years before the behind-the-scenes dialogue
of the early nineties matured into the Good Friday Agreement. At the time of writing, the collapse of the power-
sharing executive has underlined what most observers
already knew: it may again take years before that Agreement
delivers a lasting peace. As the chapters in this book dedicated to Ulster will hopefully show, the hardest struggles
are taking place in small towns where the killing had a
particularly intimate horror. When I lived in Ulster, my
encounters with politicians from the British mainland were
limited to dreary briefings at Stormont Castle or the
occasional, heavily policed walkabout in Belfast city centre.
From the point of view of many British people I met –

though they would never put it quite so crudely – Northern Ireland felt like the padded annexe in which the crazy relatives were locked away from public view.

After eighteen months in Belfast I was sent to South Africa to report the transition to democratic rule. And for the first time I began receiving large numbers of letters from British listeners. Most were appreciative and warm-hearted, and displayed a deep concern for the marginalized majority. When I made a film on the plight of a mother and her five children struggling in a squatter camp, the British public dug deep into their pockets to build her a house. Likewise in Rwanda, where the viewers of BBC 1 purchased a small herd of cows for a village decimated by the genocide. There was a palpable concern for the oppressed that crossed political boundaries; the Radio 4 audience was, politically speaking, a very broad church, united, I would suggest, by a view of the world that believes we must act according to principles of fundamental decency.

From South Africa I moved to Hong Kong to report on Asia and specifically the imminent handover of Hong Kong to the Chinese. I found myself covering wars in Afghanistan and Sri Lanka, a dictatorship of fear in Burma and the rise of authoritarian governments in South East Asia which proclaimed a new set of 'Asian values'. This involved a governing élite deciding what was best for the people, with little in the way of genuine democracy. People were certainly materially better off, but there were restrictions on press freedom and an exaggerated deference for authority. It was the era of the Asian Tiger economies, a gold rush in which there were vast profits to be made but where human rights were under constant threat.

In all, I spent nearly ten years living abroad as a BBC correspondent. Once or twice a year the BBC would fly me to London for consultations. Those crowded days were spent in a dull conference room, then at the Crown & Sceptre Pub in Portland Street and later Efe's Kebab House across the road. This was my London, a small patch of the West End through which foreign correspondents rotated at speed. The rest of Britain I didn't know at all.

During my time in South Africa and Hong Kong I'd developed a keen interest in British imperial history. The process of change unfolding in both places was a consequence of British colonialism; and so I immersed myself in the literature of the colonial age, I travelled to the battle-grounds of the Zulu and Boer wars, I visited the humid war cemeteries of Singapore, Rangoon and Hong Kong. I came from one of the conquered races, I was a child of the colonized. A large part of me revolted at the mess empires left in their wake – modern-day Burma being a case in point – yet I could not help but surrender to awe and a sneaking admiration at the breathtaking nerve it all demanded. I was present in Hong Kong to witness the last significant act of imperial retreat. By any rational judgement the notion of a colony of Chinese being ruled by a white nation thousands of miles away was anachronistic if not downright absurd. And yet the colonized were sad to see the British leave. Certainly they complained that the British had left it far too late to introduce democratic change; the pro-democracy camp felt it was being thrown to the Chinese wolves by the departing British. But when you asked ordinary Chinese people what they would miss about the British, they invariably talked about the rule of law, a sense of fair play. They felt safe with the British. It was a *feeling* rather than an intellectual position, but no less valid for that.

And then I came to live in Britain. I left Hong Kong two months after the handover. The decision to come to Britain was motivated by a growing desire to put down roots. Ten years constantly on the move can be wearing on the body and mind, not to mention the effects on a young family. When much of that time is spent in zones of conflict, there invariably comes a point when serious choices need to be made. Do you stay on the road, roaming from one war to another, an increasingly burnt-out case? Or do you find a place to call 'home' from where it is still possible to do interesting, if not necessarily life-threatening, things? In my own life, the imperative to seek a secure and sane place to live was hugely influenced by the birth of my child. In my late thirties I found myself questioning not what was good for me or my wife, but what place and country would be a fit place to raise my son and any other offspring who might come along. We took a long look around the world and for a variety of reasons, most of them practical, decided that London was the best bet. It was not an easy decision. To me, Britain was a fine place to visit for a few days; but I feared that it would suffocate me. I thought that I'd spent too long under foreign skies to settle for the tedium of domesticity in west London. The notion that Britain itself could be an 'interesting' place to report conflicted with some rather grand notions I had about myself: could I really give up the drama of the frontlines to tramp around sink estates in the north of England? What about the drama of those foreign lives in which everything happened? Coups, famines, civil wars. I decided that I would still travel out of London, but in buying a house I knew I was making a long-term commitment. I was deciding that my son would grow up with an English accent. He had been born in the last British colony in Asia and would travel on a British passport; he would grow up in London and, whether I liked it or not, his identity would in part be shaped by the children he played with, the schools he attended, the culture he absorbed. This was brought home forcefully to me when, visiting Ireland during the summer holidays, a relative announced that my son had a 'fierce English accent'. It didn't bother me, but for the first time in my life I became aware of a sense of permanence creeping into my relationship with Britain. I was going to be there for the long haul.

And so when the BBC asked me to think about making a journey through the country, I did not rush to find a foreign journey to offer as an alternative. I listened to the proposal and was intrigued. If this was the country where my child would be reared, I felt I'd better get to know something beyond the middle-class zone of comfort in which I'd settled. Over the course of nearly two years my ideas about the dullness of Britain were to be altered sharply; the stories described in this book were a vivid corrective to my foolish presumption that nothing much happened in British lives.

My previous reporting life had largely been spent trying to home in on the smaller voices locked in big conflicts. In Africa and Asia, and latterly in the Balkans, I had developed a preoccupation with the stories of the powerless. I use the word 'power' in a narrowly defined sense here: 'power' as in direct political or economic influence. They are not at all 'powerless' in the dignity they bring to the task of survival, the ingenuity with which they navigate the obstacles that spring up when you have no money or property. It is too portentous to say that I found myself *called* to such stories, perhaps it is more true to say that my instinct pulled me towards the voices of outsiders. Doubtless psychologists could argue until the cows came home about why this is the case. It doesn't really matter. For me the most vivid insights have invariably come from the mouths of those who live outside the realms of power and influence.

I have found this to be as much true of my British journey as of any I have undertaken in South Africa, the Balkans or South-East Asia. It is avowedly a journey through the country of the small voice. I began in Glasgow on a spring day, among shipyard workers who'd been told their working days were over. I finished my travels at the other end of the country, in Cornwall, in the company of a remarkable nurse, whose family history held a mirror to the struggles and sacrifices of British lives over the past one hundred years. I entered the world of the heroin addicts of Leeds, and listened to London's elderly poor speak of their remembered city; I went to the hill farms of north Wales where tenant farmers are fighting to save a way of life; and I travelled out to the western-most border of the kingdom in County Tyrone where a peace process was being threatened by the claims of the past. In Northern Ireland the issue of identity, the conflict between notions of Britishness and Irishness, is central to the narrative; though the issues of poverty are acute in many parts of the province, the overriding imperative in the lives of those I met was the outcome of the peace process. The area I visited was most definitely on the margins of Britain, and many of the people I met from both traditions expressed the feeling that they existed on the edge of national life.

In the rest of the book I have by and large avoided discussion of national identity. Nationalism has long been a personal preoccupation of mine; I have investigated what Primo Levi calls 'the bestial vice of hatred' in many countries around the world. The people I met along the road in Britain were more than capable of questioning who they were, but the different struggles they were engaged in –

feeding and educating their families, repaying crippling loans, coming down from heroin – took precedence over questions of national determinism. Of course all of these ostensibly 'bread and butter' issues have a profound effect on the idea of community, and ultimately on the question of nationhood. In the case of Scotland and Wales, the poverty I encountered has certainly been a factor in promoting disenchantment with the central government.

But in crude terms, the discourse over identity that preoccupies the political and media establishment is of little matter if you're sitting in a Govan tenement with a moneylender hammering on the door. That may seem an overly simplistic, even melodramatic, characterization of the concerns of the 'socially excluded'; I would ask you to reserve judgement until after you've read the stories of this journey.

This is above all a book of stories: the stories of British lives on the cusp of the millennium. It is written with a stranger's eye and, I hope, an open heart. Throughout the journey I was struck by the extraordinary willingness of people to lay open the most private details of their lives; so much for the legendary British 'stiff upper lip'. I can think of no more preposterous assertion than that the British have an inherent distaste for revealing their feelings. Which British, in particular, I wonder? If one reduces the stereotype still further to a notion of particularly *English* reticence, to which English are we referring? The people who live in blighted inner cities, on dying hill farms, in rural towns where the jobs have vanished? I have travelled in all of these places over the past two years and have met British people who *felt* and spoke passionately about what was happening to their lives. Very rarely did I encounter any self-pity. More often than not I was amazed by their capacity to make the best of impossible situations. I have no hesitation in describing many of them as heroes. (In a small number of cases, names have been changed to protect vulnerable people.)

When I returned to live in Britain in 1997, the country was experiencing its first year of Labour government since the 1970s. Tony Blair and his party had come to power on a promise of change, and in those autumn months of '97 the promise of a *New Britain for the New Millennium* retained a potent force. My experiences in the developing world predisposed me to a strong sympathy with any crusade to end social exclusion. I had also spent my early years on a tough council estate in north Dublin. Some of the experiences of those times are braided into the narrative of this journey; although geographically separate, the estate I briefly lived on was not at all different from those that grew up around Britain's cities in the late 1950s.

Later, in my teenage years when my family circumstances had improved, I had had the radicalizing experience of being educated by a religious brother with a fierce belief in social justice. Jerome Kelly had been called back from the missions in the West Indies to be Principal at Presentation College in Cork. The school was a bastion of the city's elite; but Jerome set about opening our eyes to a city we had never seen. It was a place where the elderly poor lived in stinking, damp hovels, scraping by on miserable pensions and the generosity of religious charities. Jerome started an organization called SHARE that raised money to build houses for the elderly poor. We were his footsoldiers, collecting on the streets and badgering businesses for contributions. He opened our eyes, and he embarrassed the political and merchant class of the city into action. Scores of houses were built in low-rise developments around the city. All of this Jerome managed without ever being morally offended by the notion of wealth, without any of the sanctimonious guff of the professional crusader. 'All I ask is that you give something back for everything you have,' he would say. It would be easy to write off such a remark as trite, were it not for the huge practical impression he made on so many lives: the lives of old people rescued from destitution, and a generation of privileged schoolboys upon whom he impressed the idea that indifference was a cardinal sin. In large measure the motivation that underpins this book, indeed much of my work, can be attributed to the influence of that good-natured, intensely practical, high-minded brother.

The Ireland of my childhood had big differences of wealth and social standing, but it did not have the historical class structure that had given the British political debate its angry subtext. As a consequence, my own political views tended to vary from issue to issue, from left to centre to right; they still do. I have never voted in a British election (I have always been abroad) and I don't support any British political party. This isn't the consequence of any moral fastidiousness or loathing of politicians. It's just not my business as a reporter to be lining up behind anybody's flag. I am certainly political, in that I believe that people who seek our votes and make promises have certain obligations. An election manifesto that promises to end social exclusion is not a wish list, it is a moral contract. My British journey took me out into the heartland of those who'd been on the receiving end of that promise. The statements they made were not overtly political, but I believe they represent a challenge to all who claim to represent the interests of the 'excluded'. My British journey was at times depressing, even frightening. More than anything, however, it was humbling and inspiring. I hope that I manage to convey at least some of the intensity of the experience in the pages that follow.

# 1. A Working Life

If you closed your eyes and listened to the noise, it was possible to imagine the world the older workers at Kvaerner described. The river in its glorious prime; a great orchestra pit out of whose depths the music of purpose swelled and echoed across the thriving yards. Fairfields, John Brown's, Harland & Wolff, Stephen's. Acres of cranes and sheds, where the piercing whistles rang three times a day declaring the turn of the shift. A 24-hour working day sliced into three parts: dayshift, backshift, nightshift. Near by were the steel works, the wire-rope manufacturers, rivet makers and a hundred more small firms that drew their living from the Clyde. They had been building ships along this river since the twelfth century. At the height of Britain's imperial glory, there were 60,000 men employed here. 'From early morn till late at night we hear the continuous hum of industry,' a local grandee had written in the middle of the nineteenth century. In two world wars the Clyde yards had been central to the defence of the realm. Battleships built on the Clyde had fought on every ocean of the world. *Clydebuilt*: a phrase spoken with pride by owners and workers alike. A byword, they said, for strength and endurance.

In 1901 three Glaswegians, writing under the pseudonym 'James Muir', described the importance of shipbuilding to the city. 'Our modern university may not impress you, the cathedral you may never see (for lack of a native to lead you to it); but our shipbuilding yards are a different matter. Before you are two days in the city you are aware of their existence; and if their importance is a matter beyond you, at least you must be impressed by our belief in it. We believe, every Glasgow man of us, that our shipbuilding is a thing to be talked of, and a most honourable and dignified business to have for the chief industry of a city.'

The Kvaerner Govan yard started life in 1864 under the name of Randolph, Elder & Company. It has been in business under one name or another ever since. In the office hallway, next to the reception area where the light filters in through a stained-glass window, there are portraits of the ships built and launched from the yard outside. My favourite is a charcoal drawing from the 1920s. There are twelve different ships as well as a submarine in the yard docks. In the foreground an ocean liner is being guided downriver by a couple of tugs and beyond the thick smoke of coal fires is rising from the Govan tenements. The whole scene is crowded with industry. One morning in the yard, I stood gazing at this picture for about ten minutes, marvelling at the detail and the energy. A man in a navy blue suit walked up. 'Those were the days, eh? We'll not see that again.'

I asked him whether he worked at the yard.

'No, thank God,' he said. And then, realizing that Morag at the front desk might be able to hear him, he added quickly: 'I don't mean that the wrong way. It's a bloody great product they make. Great. But eh, it's a wee bit too uncertain, you know. Not knowing if you're going to have a future from one week to the next. That's all I mean.'

I don't know if Morag heard us or not. She was a polite, cautious woman in her early fifties. From her desk inside the main door of Kvaerner she had watched the yard's long decline and had listed the names of all the men who'd come with bad news and of those who'd brought promises of salvation. Although I never spoke more than a few words with her, I sensed she had long ago decided to put as much faith in one as the other, which was to say she'd suspended the idea of faith.

I asked the man in blue what he did for a living. 'I'm a businessman,' he said. But he wouldn't say what his business was, nor would he give his name. I think he'd seen the word 'journalist' scrawled where I'd signed myself in just ahead of him. He was waiting to meet one of the managers. I was waiting for the Union convener. I was saved from the agonies of non-conversation by the bang of a door at the end of the hall, and the appearance of a slight figure in navy overalls and an orange hard hat. He bustled towards us with his head down. Jamie Webster.

I'd been visiting the yard for several months now and Jamie was always my first point of contact. I never knew a man to talk as much or as quickly. Before you'd even finished greeting him Jamie would launch into a detailed account of the latest negotiations. He was tireless and tiring. You could meet him first thing in the morning, feeling full of bounce, and in an hour he would have you against the ropes through sheer force of personality. Jamie was a true believer and in the early months of 1999 he was exactly what the men and women of Kvaerner needed. By the standards of the yard, he was a small man. He was thin and grey-haired with a face that *looked* permanently exhausted. But enough energy vibrated out of Jamie to hold a thousand men spellbound when he got up to speak in the works canteen. When we walked around the yard, I hurried to keep up with him. 'I'm runnin' late now. Ye'll have to talk to me on the way,' he would say, racing from one office to another, or heading down to the welding shed or fabricating shop.

His conversation invariably began with the phrase: 'Let

me tell you something.' And then he told you, without pausing to draw breath for minute after determined minute. 'God, Jamie, will you slow down,' I once pleaded. 'I cannae slow down, son. If I slow down, the whole thing slows down. We'll only survive by being one step ahead.'

I remember the first time I stood in the yard with him and listened to the sounds of the Clyde. The thrum of generators, the groan and scrape of metal sheets, the sparks of the welders' torches crackling, and a hundred unknown noises clanking and crashing along the river. It had taken us ten minutes to walk the yard. We had passed in the shadow of the cranes, lowering over us like giant question marks, and down along the river to the dockside, where the huge launching chains, links thicker than a man's arm, lay coiled amid the flotsam cast up by the river on the flood tide. Jamie pointed out the landmarks: the dry dock; the paint shed; the prefab shed where the steel is cut into the shapes demanded by the owners; the tank assembly shed where the pieces become shapes you can recognize as parts of a ship. Inside the assembly area, great pulleys moved slowly down the length of the shed, with wide sheets of steel suspended beneath them, their advance declared by the steady pulse of a high-pitched alarm. I felt Lilliputian in this landscape.

To my ears it was a powerful jumble of noise. But Jamie told me it was nothing. 'When I came in here, boy but you could feel the ground under you shaking. It was magic.' He pointed to a row of warehouses and grain stores across the river. 'That was the Glasgow port granary. That used to be full of men running about, and cranes lifting the grain out of the ships. There was ships from all over the world came in there. As a young lad I used to look across and see them, ships in from the Atlantic and the Baltic and the North Sea.'

The granaries were empty now. There were plans to turn them into riverside apartments, Jamie said.

I first met Jamie on a bright spring morning in 1999. The Kvaerner yard was in crisis again. The Norwegians who owned it had been reviewing their worldwide operations, and shipbuilding in Glasgow did not feature in their future plans. The news came in early February. A week later, news came through that the Arctic Survey boat they'd been depending on was going to another yard. Kvaerner announced they were getting out and wanted a buyer. The absence of any big order made it a less than attractive proposition.

Jamie Webster had entered the yards as a sixteen-year-old, following his da's advice to get a trade. His father had run a grocer's shop and didn't see a future for his son behind the counter. Jamie suspects he was a Conservative voter. I joked that he'd had the same shopkeeper background as Margaret Thatcher. Jamie told me it was the only similarity. He wasn't the first union man or Kvaerner employee to use the doleful phrase: *at least with her you knew who the enemy was.* The men of Kvaerner were living in a world where the old enemy had been vanquished. Yet they found themselves on the threshold of closure. The party that had been founded as the voice of the working man was in power. But in those early months of 1999 it didn't seem to make any difference. Barring a miracle – a sudden big order or the sale of the yard as a going concern – Kvaerner were going to shut up shop.

Jamie had been around the yards long enough to know what the threat of closure did to men. The slow erosion of morale, the look of defeat that came into their eyes, the incremental departure of hope as negotiations went nowhere. His first job had been at the Barley Curle yard across the river. That lasted a year before the closure notice went up. But it was 1967, and there were still other yards in which to find work. He remembered men taking their redundancy pay and starting up the following day somewhere else along the river. He himself came across to what would later become Kvaerner. There were 4,000 men working there back then. 'My brother had been in the yard for a year, but he quit. It wasn't for him. You see all those big walls, to him that was like a prison. But it's no like that to me. This is my second home. When I came in here I was a boy and there was all these big men, tough characters, and you sure as anything didn't want to be a shrinking violet around them boys. The humour in here was, still can be, very rough at times. If you have any wee thing noticeable about ye, they're on to it. The banter never stops. You'd have to have that in an industry as tough as this. Men died in these yards, remember, it's a dangerous industry. People fell or were crushed or got burned.'

He reeled off a list of names. The Pig. The Paratrooper. Pinky and Perky. Nicknames. He smiled then and told me a story about a man who was taken ill in the yard a few years back. 'Right away the boys called an ambulance, comforted him and made sure he was looked after. The ambulance came and everybody waited on word from the hospital. See, as soon as it came, the word starts goin' round. "Where does he keep his sandwiches?" Everybody knew his wife made great sandwiches. So there was no sentimentality about eating them once he was out of sight!'

Jamie was forty-nine years of age and had spent all his adult working life in the yard. When he told me what he was paid, I did a double take: £200 a week. And that was *with* overtime. After thirty-three years in the yard Jamie Webster was barely earning £10,000 a year after tax. There was a 37-hour week and a three-week holiday in August when the yard had its annual shut-down. But ten grand a year was as good as it got. Jamie knew there were young men working in the City of London who'd feel insulted if they were offered a ten grand bonus at the end of the year. If he'd been watching television that night he'd have seen a London estate agent being presented with a BMW convertible as a reward for high sales figures. Yet I never had the feeling that Jamie felt resentment or that he felt society owed him anything. What he wanted was to hold on to a job he still loved. It was that which pushed him towards union activism, not politics or ambition. Jamie knew from the outset he wasn't cut out for high union office. Yard convener, that was as far as he was going or wanted to go. In 1967 – the same year Jamie came into the yards – Harold Wilson's government proposed amalgamating all of the Upper Clyde shipyards. That was Brown's, Connel's, Stephen's, Fairfield's and Yarrow. The group was called the Upper Clyde Shipbuilders. By 1971 the venture had collapsed, and the Upper Clyde Shipbuilders went into liquidation. In July the workers began a fight to save their jobs. They staged a work-in which went on through the year. The result was another merger, which brought the Govan Shipbuilders Company into being. But the decline in the worldwide shipping market continued; the age of glory on the Clyde was long since gone, and the yard was only saved when it was nationalized by Jim Callaghan's government in 1977.

Jamie was married and had three children by this stage. He was beginning to worry that the yard and his job were doomed. 'I was starting to listen to the trade union officials and realized the decline was really getting serious. Two small yards left out of sixteen. I wouldn't say it sneaked up on us. But sometimes you can get a bit selfish. You watch another yard go and say, "Thank God it's not us." It visited our door a few times, the threat of closure. But you survive and go on, and that gives you a kind of confidence until the next big threat comes along.'

The threat bearing down now was arguably the most ominous in the yard's history. Unless Kvaerner found a buyer by the middle of summer – just four months away – the 1,200 men and women who worked at the Govan yard would lose their livelihoods.

The shipbuilders battled to compete with the cheaper competition from Asian and other European shipyards; these yards, according to the Govan men, received stronger support from their governments. But they didn't labour the political points; at the end of the twentieth century there was no public sympathy for the idea of major state inter-vention to save dying industry. A big dole-out of taxpayers' money was not on the cards. The unions could pressure government, and government could coax and cajole poten-tial buyers. The possibility of government orders for new ships was dangled before prospective buyers but never guaranteed. Everything was tentative. At the back of workers' minds was the continual worry that a takeover might just be a prelude to the break-up of the company.

I used to follow the progress of the Kvaerner story from London. Not that it made much news in the capital. The story fitted into an outdated template. Dying industry, unions fighting against closure, local politicians expressing concern. Britain had seen so many of these stories during the recessions of the seventies and eighties; in an age of growth and generally falling unemployment, such a crisis, indeed the whole notion of heavy industry itself, seemed an anachronism. The fact that 1,200 people, most of them with families, would be turned from productive members of society into welfare statistics failed to grip the imagination of the public. Perhaps we assumed that in a general age of prosperity unemployment could never last for long. The shipyard men would be *all right*.

A man like Davy McCuish would have been inclined to take a different view. Davy was the son of a former shipyard worker, and he hadn't had a full-time job for five years. He and his pal Bill went into Brechins some days after being down the Programme Centre. Davy swore by the pint in Brechins. It's a gloomy cavern of a place halfway up the Govan Road. In the main downstairs bar, a television blasted out non-stop sport. Below it clusters of men sat with pints, some staring at the screen, others drifting in and out of conversation. Nobody bothered you if you wanted to sit alone with a pint. Govan might have a rough name, but in Brechins you didn't annoy your neighbour. A sign warned that customers who were barred should not try to gain entry, lest refusal would offend them or their families. I had the strong sense that causing offence to a troublesome customer would be well down the list of the owner's worries. Ironically Brechins had started life as a hall for temperance workers in the 1890s. With time the power of drink overcame the attractions of piety and the stern lectures of the teetotallers were replaced by the hubbub of drinking men. Hard drinking and its sorrowful consequences have a long history in Govan.

The working-class Glasgow of the turn of the century is described powerfully in the novels of Patrick MacGill, who emigrated from County Donegal to Scotland at that time. MacGill came as a potato picker and ended up a celebrated novelist, a good-luck story in a city where thousands were stranded in poverty. His books *The Rat-Pit* and *Children of the Dead End* are no longer widely read. It is a pity, because his observations of life in the slums are heart-stopping. In *The Rat-Pit* he describes a young emigrant girl, pregnant and unmarried, wandering through the streets in search of her friend.

Norah travelled through the streets all day, looking for her friend and fearing that every eye was fixed on her, that everybody knew the secret she tried to conceal. Her feet were sore, her breath came in short, sudden gasps as she took her way into dark closes and climbed creaking stairs . . . here in the poorer parts of the city, in the crooked lanes and straggling alleys, were dirt, darkness and drunkenness. A thousand smells greeted the nostrils, a thousand noises grated on the ears; lights flared brightly in the beershops; fights started at the corners; ballad singers croaked out their songs; intoxicated men fell in the gutters.

It's bleak stuff, and MacGill's anger at the conditions he encountered is palpable. That crowded Glasgow has now vanished. The streets are clean today. The crooked lanes and straggling alleys have given way to wide-open thoroughfares and vast housing estates. The city of rickets and tuberculosis is gone. There is money in the air and new buildings are going up along the Clyde. At the end of a day in Govan I would drive through the Clyde Tunnel to a world of new hotels and luxury flats, shopping centres and multiplex cinemas. It was like switching from black and white to colour television.

Sometimes in the afternoon Davy McCuish walked down to the Clyde to spend an hour or so looking at the men working on the new buildings. His da had worked in the yards. He came back from the army in 1950 and walked straight into a job in Fairfield's. Like many men in those days he worked in most of the Clyde yards at one time or another. Davy remembers a house where there was a strong work ethic and enough money to get by on. The shipyard, the army and the dying empire they served – all were woven through the stories of Davy's childhood. His paternal grandfather was wounded on the Western Front, shot thirty-six times in the back. That was how his father learned to count, counting the scars in the old man's back. He was fifty-seven when he died of complications caused by the old wounds.

Davy shared a bedroom with his maternal grandfather. He'd joined the navy and was present when the *Graf Spee* was sunk at the River Plate. His name was James but the family called him 'Old Jamaica', after the rum. After the war he went into the merchant navy and sailed the world. At night, lying in bed, he would regale Davy with stories of his journeys and, as the boy got older, boast of his conquests in foreign ports. When he tells you about those days you see a different Davy. The cynical mask slips and the face of a much younger man is revealed. He smiles and gestures, summoning back the image of the old sailor blathering the night away, while his mother called out to the two of them to shut up and go to sleep. One night a gale blew up the Clyde and down the chimney into their bedroom. 'The two of us were sat in the bed and covered in soot. Black as the ace of spades. And we laughed I can tell you. What else could we do but sit there laughing?' But the old man drank heavily and he couldn't get on with his daughter. And after one ferocious row he left. 'Old Jamaica' ended up in a centre for down and outs, where he died when Davy was fourteen years of age. He helped carry the coffin at the funeral.

The two world wars in which Davy's grandfathers served

had provided stays of execution for the Clyde yards. With the demand for battleships to fight the Kaiser and then Hitler, production and the consequent need for labour surged. But the wars distorted the truth of the shipbuilding economy. The real story from the turn of the century onwards was of steady decline along the Clyde. Between the wars the Clyde yards faced disaster: during 1933, in the middle of the depression, the Clyde produced just 50,000 tons of shipping, about one fifth of its capacity. Unemployment along the river soared to 25 per cent. I tried to bear this in mind on Sunday mornings when I listened to the older people, sitting over a cup of tea in the community hall at the Pearse Institute, recalling the busy streets of old Govan. There had never been a time when their days weren't circumscribed by the fear of sudden closure. Govan had enjoyed no golden age in living memory; its story was the story of Britain's imperial and industrial decline. There were periods of respite, but, as the century progressed, they became fewer and thinner. Still the old people would be fond of telling you that they knew they would never go hungry. Somebody always had a pot of soup and shared it out; and people kept an eye on each other's kids. Not like now, they endlessly reminded you.

By the time Davy came out of school in the mid seventies, the Clyde was a river of ghosts. There was no walking straight into a job in the yards. Davy had been in and out of work ever since. More out than in. Fifteen years of part-time jobs. His first marriage went by the wayside because of unemployment, he says. He was depressed and put his wife and three kids through a hard time. Actually, he says, he put them through hell. But he doesn't elaborate. The kids from that marriage are all teenagers now and he sees them regularly. He remarried five years ago and has three young children: two boys aged five and one, and a three-year-old girl. Sometimes at night he goes into the kids' bedroom and watches them while they are asleep. And then the guilt gets hold of him and he starts thinking how useless he is and how he's letting them down. His last job had seemed like a sure thing, working as the document checker for a transport firm. He liked the work, checking if the licences and tax of the cars and vans were up to date. But the firm was taken over and Davy lost out. He had the feeling that bad luck followed him to every job he tried. And nagging away inside him was the knowledge that he was the first man in his family to queue up in a benefit office.

Meeting him for the first time you could be put off by his bitterness. It filled up the small sitting room of his flat with tension, leaving you grappling for the right words to end the silence. He would snap at the kids or his wife, and I had the feeling that a lot of the time they were wary around him. The relentless cynicism was, I suspect, his defence against the charges he hurled at himself: the jobless man of the house, the father who failed his children, the man who wasn't a man. His days were a model of orderly emptiness. He'd get up and take the kids to school before meeting up with his friend Bill and going to the Programme Centre across in Mosspark Boulevard. It took them about half an hour to get there. After the centre they might go for a pint or he'd go back home and watch television. In the afternoons he walked by the river before going back up Govan Road to collect the kids. On Monday nights he went to play dominoes at the Rangers Supporters' Club. His only other outings were when he played the turntable at discos around Govan. He was rewarded for his services with free drinks. And that was it, every week of the year.

One morning I went with Davy and his mate Bill to the Programme Centre over in Mosspark. He didn't have much enthusiasm for the trip. If he didn't go, didn't show he was making the effort, he could lose his benefit. But he knew by now that his chances of getting a permanent job were small. Out of the thousand who went to the centre in a year, fewer than half got jobs. The idea was that unemployed men and women would come in and look for jobs in the centre's newspapers and on the wall notices. There were a couple of phones, a photocopying machine, a few tables and some smiling staff. A notice reminded the unemployed that they needed to spend an hour and a half on the premises before they could claim travel expenses. It was a small modern office, all bright paint and positivity. SELL YOUR-SELF commanded a notice inside the door. Another sign offered jobs at Chubb Security for £3.75 an hour. BRAE-HEAD — BE PART OF SCOTLAND'S BIGGEST EVER RETAIL AND LEISURE DEVELOPMENT. 3,000 VACANCIES . . . declared another.

Davy dialled several numbers and asked for application forms. He checked up on jobs he'd applied for the previous week. I watched his expression as he told them who he was and waited. He made four calls. In the end he turned to me and shrugged. Nothing doing, he said. He and Bill sat down at a table and read the newspapers. Bill had worked in the yards and been made redundant about seven years before. Having no job made him feel like he was nothing, he said. There were six other people in the room doing the same thing. Sitting looking at the papers and waiting to pass the hour and a half so they'd get the travel expenses. The manager of the centre was a short, energetic man called John Boland. There were people who'd been twenty to thirty years unemployed, he said. They'd lost out in the recessions and spent the rest of their lives trying to get started again. The longer you were out of a job, the less likely an employer would be to have any interest in you. Most of the jobs on offer were in the service sector – barmen, waiters, security guards, shop assistants – and they generally paid the minimum wage, £3.60 an hour. If you worked a 37-hour week that would leave you with £133.20 a week before tax. All the old engineering jobs were going, according to John. Welding was a dying industry, even plumbers were in trouble. What you had happening a lot now was marine engineers and such applying for jobs as waiters and security guards. It's depressing, said John. He'd been an engineer working for the old Glasgow firm of Montgomery Engineering. When the factory closed four years ago he'd done a lot of different jobs before getting the job at the Programme Centre. John reckoned that if you were aged between twenty-five and thirty-nine you had a good enough chance of getting a job. But the younger applicants, and the older ones, were in trouble. After half an hour in the centre, Davy and Bill got up and went for a pint.

Davy knew a lot of men who worked at Kvaerner. I often wondered what they made of him, what they thought when they saw what was becoming of his life. Did they think to themselves: *That's me if the yard goes. I can become that man hauling his memories and his anger from the riverbank to the Programme Centre to Brechins.* I know that plenty of them were sick with worry about what the death of the yard would do to them, their families, their way of life. And when I watched their battle to save the yard, followed its passion and fierce determination, I sensed the workers had both eyes firmly fixed on that other-world of waste and shrinking that hovered like a promise just outside the gates.

# 2. Out There

You could take a hundred poverty reports, digest a million statistics, and they wouldn't tell you as much as one walk down the Govan Road, a road you could walk on the finest summer's day, with the sunlight flooding across the tenement roofs, and still remember it only in black and white. It has less to do with what you see than with the aura of palpable absences that hangs over the place.

I remembered what an old woman had told me about waiting for her dad on the corner after work, and how the road would fill with thousands of men as soon as the yard horns sounded. Her father would watch through the legs of the other men, scanning the side of the street for his daughter's skinny knees. And when he reached her, he would hoist her above the crowd to see the road thick with people flooding towards the Cross. These days the shipyard worker going to and from work, or heading out to buy a paper or a packet of fags at lunchtime, would see an empty road and wonder if his job would go the way of those vanished men.

It is a walk of about seven minutes from the shipyard gate up to Govan Cross. The first thing you see outside the yard is a TO LET sign on an old minicab office; next to that a fast-food store; and then the Cheque Centre, where cheques are cashed, loans advanced and the telephone lines open eight to eight. *Instant cash* is the promise. Then there is a bookie's, a Chinese takeaway, Coburn's Undertakers and the Cheap and Cheerful Charity Shop. In the window of the last is a sign condemning the hooligans who broke in and stole a pile of old clothes: *Congratulations to the brave people who broke in here and stole from those less fortunate than themselves.* The shop stands on the corner of Howatt Street with its great red-brick tenements and a mural of working men painted on to the shipyard wall at the end of the street. Keep going on up the Govan Road and you pass a line of boarded-up buildings. Among them is a baker's shop, a few derelict tenement flats and then more of the little offices promising instant cash and easy loans.

On the corner of Howatt Street stood a man with a huge dog. It looked like a cross between an Alsatian and a polar bear. 'What breed is that?' I asked. He mentioned a Japanese name and told me not to worry. It wouldn't attack unless he gave the word. Why did he need something that big?

''Cos there's some right bad bastards around here is why,' he replied. As we were talking, a man came out of the Cheap and Cheerful Charity Shop. He introduced himself as Brian and said he was the manager.

'Did you hear about last night?' he asked. 'A girl livin' behind there' – he pointed across the street – 'stabbed her man.'

The man with the dog said he'd seen the police around the place. I asked what it was all about.

'Apparently he was an alcoholic. He came back from the pub and started batterin' her and she stabbed him in the heart.' He conveyed this information in a matter-of-fact voice. 'It's the second boyfriend she's done this to,' he added.

I asked whether the other had been a drunk too.

'I don't know. Probably.'

'Fuck me, I'll be sure not to go home with her,' said the man with the dog.

As we stood talking, a queue was forming outside the building next door. The man with the dog said they were all people trying to get their money sorted. Most of those in the queue were women. Above the door of the building was a sign saying, MONEY MATTERS.

Brian from Cheap and Cheerful said the Money Matters people were dead decent. They helped sort out people's benefit hassles and interceded for them with the loan companies. The window was covered with posters offering advice on disability and unemployment benefits. At ten o'clock the door opened and the queue shuffled inside. I followed them in and introduced myself to a girl called Jackie behind the desk. The manager would be in shortly, she said. Would I mind waiting a few minutes?

Jackie moved along the line of people, offering each a form on which they were to fill in the essential details of their lives. Names, Addresses, Financial Problems.

An old man came in, stumbling through the doorway. I thought at first he might be drunk, but then saw the thick glasses and squinting eyes – he could barely see. Jackie took his hand and led him to a seat. He was seventy-six years old and his name was Jack. Jack's clothes were covered in old food stains, and he smelled of urine. There was a problem with his electricity bill. All of a sudden it had jumped from £26 to £84. One of the older workers at the centre, a woman in her fifties, came out and ushered him into an alcove. There Jack described what had happened. The bill was an estimate because he was afraid to let people into the house. You never knew if it was someone wanting to break in and attack you. 'What about your neighbours? Couldn't you have got them to do it?' the woman asked. 'I don't trust them. They're all fly-by-nights,' he replied. The woman walked to another part of the office and picked up the phone to the electricity people. The person on the other end of the line was reasonable. They would look into it immediately. The old man wasn't to worry.

Next in line was a woman called Jeanette. She had four children and was living in her sister's council flat. It was crowded but better than the bed and breakfast they'd spent months in. Jeanette's husband was *gone*. I would hear that word often on my journey. *Gone*. It could mean a lot of things. *Gone* as in he upped and vanished without saying a word. *Gone* as in he wrecked the place, beat me up and I got a barring order. *Gone* meaning he was too out of it or off his head to get any sense from. *Gone* meaning he was dead from drink or drugs and definitely wouldn't be returning. In Jeanette's case he had simply vanished. The council had given her five camp beds and a fridge. But she had benefit and debt trouble. Now she was hoping Money Matters would help her sort all this out and get them a house to live in.

The waiting room was filling up quickly. A young couple came in with a toddler. The man had a long scar across his right eye. The woman was telling him he should give up smoking. 'It's bad for the child. If ye can't do it for yourself, do it for her.' And then she became aware of the quiet in the room, sensed that every ear in the place, including mine, was tuned in to the argument. She turned her face away from the man and drew her nose gently up and down the baby's cheek. The three of them walked to the end of the bench and sat down. There were two other women there and a young woman who looked like an outsider. That is, someone who didn't look pale and exhausted and nervous. It later turned out she worked for a firm of solicitors who were helping Money Matters.

After about twenty minutes a middle-aged blonde

woman strode into the waiting area. 'Good morning all,' she announced. Only Jeanette replied. 'Hiya Geraldine.' The others nodded.

Geraldine McCaskill was the manager. At forty years of age she might by now have expected to be enjoying a management role in a comfortable office somewhere in central Glasgow. Geraldine had been an official in the Council Housing Office when, in 1990, her bosses had asked if she'd like to work out in the community. They had a simple problem. Rent arrears were creeping up. As council tenants in places like Govan got deeper in debt with loan companies, they were defaulting on their rent. The idea of Money Matters was to sit people down and help them to reorganize their finances so that they paid what they could. Pretty soon people were flooding in with queries and problems.

Geraldine had some idea of the territory. Her family had originally come from the Gorbals. In the sixties they moved out to a housing scheme called Castlemilk on the south side. Eight of them shared a two-bedroom house. She, her mother, father and brother shared one bedroom; her aunt, gran and two sisters the other. The Castlemilk Estate was supposed to be a big improvement for the people of the Gorbals. The problem was that while the Council built flats, there were precious few amenities to go with them. But the family was better off than most. Geraldine's father worked on the railways and her mother raised the children. Both parents had fairly strict ideas about borrowing. You didn't do it if you could possibly avoid it. You spent what you had and no more. And you always paid your bills. A treat was a jam piece – a piece of bread with jam on it. Holidays were a free trip on the railways to some seaside town.

Such an upbringing might, you think, have given Geraldine McCaskill little tolerance for the legion of bad debtors and welfare dependants who queued ceaselessly outside her office. But Geraldine had listened to too much misery to make any condemnation; nor, it has to be said, was she inclined to rant against the iniquities of government or the council. Her business was the work of sorting out the messy, complicated, bureaucratic tangles that poor people fell into. Geraldine called them 'clients'. It was a phrase that I felt maintained a necessary illusion: that the people outside were not dependent, that they had picked this little office out of a multitude of choices. As we were talking the room outside filled up with clients. Most of Geraldine's staff were young welfare rights officers. I was struck by the gentleness of their approach. They *listened*.

People came to Money Matters literally weeping with worry. They might owe hundreds or thousands in rent arrears; on top of that there were catalogue loans or hire-purchase deals or the money owed to instant loan companies. The interest rates on a typical loan could run to 50 per cent or more. That was with the relatively 'generous' companies. There were others that offered goods on hire purchase for, say, £500 and then collected repayments of £1,500. And if you couldn't pay, the store's heavies arrived and removed the furniture. You owned nothing until you made the final payment. Default, and your precious furniture went.

At the very bottom of the scale were the moneylenders who operated outside any laws of decency. You failed to repay them, and they started by taking your goods. Then they moved on to bodily harm. The loan companies operated entirely within the laws of the land. The law allowed them to charge poverty-stricken people huge rates of interest. And the people didn't complain because they needed the loan companies. Just ask yourself if American

Express or Visa or Diners' Club would entertain an application from a welfare-dependent citizen of Govan.

Geraldine had to deal with the loan companies on a regular basis and so in our conversations she generally avoided criticizing them. But she told me she'd actually heard a loan company advise a debtor to borrow more money to get out of their present fix. 'They prey on these people. They encourage them to go in deeper. You're talking about people who have nowhere else to go. They can't go to banks, they don't have collateral to offer. What do you have to offer if you're on benefit? So they get in deeper and deeper. And if you don't have anything for your kids coming up to Christmas, you don't think of the end result of borrowing or how long it's going to take to pay it off. You can survive on benefit, but it leaves nothing extra for a pair of new shoes, or school uniforms, or any kind of crisis. There are people who say it's all their own fault. I'd say to them: "You try living on benefit." They could do it short term but long term they'd find it extremely difficult.' Geraldine reckons that she could do a great deal more. But her funding has been cut and cut. It isn't that her operation has been deliberately targeted, but that the council has made cuts across the board. As the council has slashed thousands from her budget, so staff have had to be let go. To keep the operation going in any meaningful way, she's had to go to the private sector. She doesn't ask for charity, but offers Money Matters expertise to companies who want their staff to learn sound financial management. Some twenty thousand people a year seek the help of Geraldine and her staff, not to mention those who are visited in their own homes or who hear the message delivered by the Money Matters people when they tour local schools. On one level the values of Money Matters are decidedly old-fashioned:

you pay your bills, you learn how to prioritize your spending. But the trick of it, and what keeps people crowding through the front door, is that nobody in Money Matters lectures the poor. *Clients*, not supplicants.

In more than a year of talking to people on welfare, I never met one who said they couldn't *survive* on benefit. But that was the extent of it. *Survive*. There was just about enough to put food on the table and pay the rent and heating bills. But even the best budgeters couldn't avoid going into debt when Christmas came around or a child's birthday loomed. I had started out in Govan with a suitcase full of prejudice. I used to look at their children, often dressed in expensive trainers and sweatsuits, playing with computer games or watching satellite television, and question the idea that they were suffering from poverty.

And then, as the months went on, as I travelled down through Britain and the nature of the choices poor people faced was revealed, I learned to be more cautious. This was a world where you had to ask yourself every day: how would I survive down here? A week or two as an entertaining social experiment, oh fine. A few MPs have tried it with camera crews in tow. But the soul-numbing, every-day-of-the-year, relentless grind of it? I knew I would sink very quickly. The government's own figures, if you took time to read them, were a swift antidote to prejudice. They told you that fewer than half of working-age council tenants had jobs, that Scottish children faced one of the highest risks of growing up in poverty anywhere in the EU (one in four lived in homes dependent on income support), that a third of Scottish pensioners had no source of income other than state pensions.

A long time ago, I had hovered on the edge of that world.

At the beginning of the 1960s my parents came back from England to live in Dublin. The country was just starting to get moving again after the economic depression of the forties and fifties. A lot of people were giving up jobs in London and Birmingham and going home. My parents had no money and were living on a huge council estate on the outskirts of the city. There was a village near by with a few shops, a chippy and several pubs.

Finglas was not unlike many of the estates that had been built around the big towns of Britain in the years after the Second World War. The Dublin town planners had taken a look at the green fields of north County Dublin and decided that urban sprawl was the answer to their problems. And people who'd been crammed into miserable tenements were happy to be going there. For kids who'd lived with the grime and roar of the inner city, the green fields of Finglas were a wild frontier. As the building went on, the fields disappeared. Hard men from the tenements of the inner city found themselves transported into fresh concrete avenues that bore the names of dead Irish patriots. We lived on Casement Green, named after Roger Casement, who'd been hanged for treason after trying to smuggle guns into Ireland in the uprising of 1916. My old neighbour Breda Thunder describes it as a place of great equality. 'Everybody had fuck all and we shared it around.' Her husband Liam had worked on the buses in Birmingham before coming back and starting up his own bread-round. His brother was off with the Irish Guards in Aden. Lots of people had relatives in England who were sending money home.

The joke was that Finglas was so tough even the Alsatians went around in pairs. In 1961 my father and mother arrived there by taxi; what they owned fitted easily into the boot and back seat. Some books and clothes, a few ornaments. It was my father's habit to spend what he earned on drink. And when the money ran out, he would pawn whatever came to hand. When he ran out of things to pawn, he turned to moneylenders. In those years debt collectors of one kind or another would constantly pitch up at the front door demanding payment. My mother was saved by Breda Thunder, who acted as unpaid childminder. She looked after my brother and myself while my mother went out to work. Bit by bit my mother paid off the debt collectors until at last they left us in peace.

I have one recurring memory of those days. Months had gone by without rent being paid, and we eventually got a summons to appear in court. My mother took me with her to Kilmainham District Court. I remember that her hand was shaking in mine as we climbed the steps into the building. The judge was kind and listened patiently to our tale of woe. My mother was not the kind of person he expected to see before him for rent arrears. She was a teacher and she came from the middle classes. Maybe that influenced his attitude to us. He dismissed the case on condition that my mother made regular payments to clear the arrears. But I can't forget, ever, the fear on my mother's face as we walked into that courtroom. She had no power and we both knew it.

There were plenty of women on that estate whose husbands drank the wages, or who simply couldn't or wouldn't get a job. There was a woman up the road who left her kids with the neighbours and took the early bus into town to clean offices and schools. She had a couple of young boys and her husband was a drunk. You never saw much of him, but the sons were wild. The Guards were always around to the house. They were the kind of boys you didn't need to be warned to stay away from. Some kind of feral cunning told you these boys would always take it further than you ever wanted to go. They might set fire to things or throw rocks through people's windows. And they'd go down the shops stealing or out to where the new houses were being built so they could nick shovels when the workmen weren't looking. Their mother left and returned in the dark. You'd catch sight of the husband around midday, heading down to the village. What we knew for certain is that they were a lot worse off than us. However bad things were, we weren't as bad as that. We knew we were middle-class people trapped in this slice of urban bleakness. We were made for better things. My mother had qualifications and determination, and told us we would escape from that world. And when the creditors are knocking on your front door, that little sliver of difference between you and the crowd across the way can look like wide blue ocean.

Even in the last chance saloon that was Money Matters, there was a descending scale of the beleaguered. Right down at the bottom, in a mess so deep she couldn't see the vaguest chink of light, was a thin, red-haired woman called 'Marie'. The first time I met Marie, she was sitting in Geraldine's office with tears streaming down her face. Someone told me she was only thirty, but she looked like a woman in her mid forties. Marie was an old client of Money Matters, but Geraldine still hadn't been able to find out how much she owed. It could have been that Marie no longer knew. There was money owed to the DSS on a social loan; money owed to a loan company and a catalogue firm; arrears of rent. And there were rumours of moneylenders in the background. She'd been blacklisted by the loan companies, so she raised credit by getting a friend to take out loans. People did it all the time. Marie juggled the debts. The DSS loan and council arrears were deducted at source. One week the loan company got paid, another week the catalogue people. At the end of it all Marie had £72 a week for herself and her two young boys. And out of that came food and heating and electricity and telephone, and children's birthday and Christmas presents and clothes.

Marie had been born in Howatt Street in the shadow of the shipyard. On both sides, her people had come over from Ireland. Her father's family had emigrated to Glasgow at the time of the Irish Civil War in 1923. They left a shattered Irish Free State for the tenements of Glasgow and the promise of work in the factories of the Clyde. Her mother's people were from Belfast, and they'd followed the old migration route across the northern channel. Her granda had found work in the shipyards. He was there for the boom years of the Second World War and his son – Marie's father – followed him into the yard. Her dad qualified as an insulation engineer and her brother had worked there too. Both lost their jobs in the eighties. But she had grown up in a house where both parents had worked. Her mother was a secretarial assistant and taught typing in her spare time. There was nothing in that early childhood to forewarn of a life of dependency and debt.

After her father lost his job he still got up every morning as if he were going to start an early shift in the yard. But over time he began to head instead to the pubs. His drinking got worse and after a while he was no longer welcome in the pubs. He took to drinking on the street corner opposite Money Matters. Marie would see him often as he walked up the Govan Road. He would stand with the other alcoholics and drink whiskey out of a can. 'I used to meet him on the street but I couldn't tell him what to do. There was no talking him out of it. He was a good man went to waste.'

One night he went mad in the house and Marie's brother dragged him out the back and beat him up before calling the police. After that her father moved out. First he stayed with her grandmother and aunt, then he found a flat of his own, and then he found his way to a bed for alcoholics in hospital, where he died.

Marie was his favourite. The youngest child who still missed him terribly. She made excuses for him. It was the people he drank with. They were a bad influence. Once he lost his job he was naturally going to do the same as the others who hung around drinking all the time. If he hadn't lost his job things would have been different. Maybe they would have. There were plenty of men who fell to drink as a full-time occupation once their daily purpose had been taken away.

Marie lived in Drumoyne, in what was once regarded as one of the better parts of Govan. When I went to visit her the bulldozers were at work on the block of flats across the way. Drumoyne was being 'regenerated'. In a few months' time new buildings would rise from the mound of bricks and smashed glass and timber. The flat blocks were low rise, two floors and fronted with solid grey stone. They must have seemed like a deliverance to the people who came here from overcrowded tenements in the fifties. But walk down Drumoyne now and into Duthill Street and you'll see broken windows and scorched interiors where the abandoned flats have been burned out by gangs of bored teenagers; you'll see the same teenagers sitting in stairwells watching you pass, going quiet when you approach. They are sizing you up. A well-dressed stranger could be many things here. He could be from the DSS or maybe looking for truants. A drugs squad cop would be unlikely to ramble around on his own like that. Another possibility was that he was a Jehovah's Witness or a Mormon come to save the immortal souls of Govan's poor.

I was afraid of these kids. At any moment they could have robbed me or beaten me up. But though they saw me pass many times they never said a word. After I'd passed I would hear the voices start up again, a dislocated clamour that ricocheted around the empty building. Once, coming down the street, I was approached by two middle-aged men. One had long unkempt hair and badly rotting teeth; the other was short, stocky and dressed in a clean tracksuit. The tracksuited one had a small girl in tow, a daughter I assumed. What was I doing here, they wanted to know? I explained what I was doing and asked if they had jobs. 'Jobs fuck. There's no jobs here. There's plenty drugs, though,' said the man with the bad teeth. The two of them laughed. Then the man in the tracksuit said he'd been in the army in Germany but had been invalided out because of a problem with his leg. He couldn't get a job and lived on disability benefit. The girl was his niece and he was minding her while her mother went into town. They were friendly. In fact, I didn't meet a single person in Govan who wouldn't talk or who reacted defensively. They were past all that.

Right in front of where Marie lived was a square of green parkland. I never saw it when it wasn't flooded. People dumped big plastic bags full of rubbish into the water, and they floated like bloated bodies amid the other detritus: a punctured leather football, a rusting supermarket trolley, a child's bicycle.

Marie lived on the second floor of a block of flats that was being redecorated by the council. On the first afternoon I visited, the two boys were still at school. There was a large picture portrait of them just above the electric fire in the sitting room. Billy, aged ten, and his brother Jack, aged six. Both had their mother's red hair. They smiled in the photograph. It was the only place or circumstance in which I would ever see them smile. The boys had two different fathers. Billy's dad had been a local heavy, or, in Marie's words, he was a Jekyll and Hyde type. All over you one minute, beating the shite out of you the next. She didn't know where he was now and didn't care as long as he was out of her life. Jack's dad was Andy, who was a more gentle type. He lived around the corner and they often had their tea at his house.

There was damp on the walls of Marie's flat and a wide dark stain on her bedroom ceiling where the rain came through. But I'd seen worse places. It was the sense of defeat that really closed in after you'd spent any time with Marie. That first afternoon she spoke about the debt and how she'd lost track of how much she owed and to whom she owed it. There was self-pity in her voice, but you couldn't hold it against her. Things were as bad as she described. Why didn't she go and get a job? In the beginning she had worked, she said. There was a job in a shop and a couple of cleaning jobs. Then she got pregnant and went on to benefit. By the time she had her son the father had vanished and she was left to worry about childcare on her own. Had Marie gone out and got a full-time job it would just about have paid for a childminder. What was the point? You could talk about work ethic and pride and all that, but in the end it came down to simple economics. If you are a parent who has to pay for childcare, then low-paid jobs are like no jobs at all. And that was the beginning of Marie's trap.

By the time I met her, I doubt she could have held down a job with even the most tolerant employer. Her nerves were stretched too far for a normal job. In the middle of a conversation, she would drift off and start staring at a point on the wall. The smallest aggravation would set her shaking. She had a small dog, a Yorkshire terrier, which she held close to her cheek as she spoke. When she got upset and started to cry, the dog licked her face. Marie had a daydream that she was standing on the Govan Road and a millionaire stopped in a big car and invited her to sit inside. He carried her away in his car and gave her all the money she needed. She was able to pay off her loans and buy the kids everything they wanted. At last she was able to stop feeling as if she were the worst mother in the world. She smiled when she said that.

A few months later I came back to seek her out and see if anything had changed. It took days to make contact. Geraldine at Money Matters told me she'd been calling and leaving messages, but Marie hadn't responded. 'We can help her with the debt if she'll just get in touch.' But there was silence.

There was a rumour doing the rounds that Marie had borrowed £40 from a moneylender to get her through Christmas. She'd failed to pay up and the woman had come round and beaten her up. Now she had a fortnight to find the money or she'd get a worse beating. I eventually tracked her down at the gates of her younger son's school. Marie went there every afternoon to pick him up. She was apologetic when we met. 'I'm just runnin' about doin' this and that. You know how it is, how busy you can get. And I had a flu over Christmas and I'm just over it.' The young boy raced ahead of us, as we walked back towards the flat. He pulled some berries from a hedge and ran back, pelting us as he came. He screamed at his mother and took his coat off, throwing it on the ground. She smiled and tried to placate him, but it made no difference. After a few minutes he picked up the coat and ran ahead of us again, repeating the tantrum every hundred yards or so.

Back in the flat her elder son was watching television. He looked at me, said nothing and walked out. I tried to ask Marie a few more questions about her background. She got as far as telling me that her brother and two sisters had all done well for themselves. They lived in 'bought' houses and had jobs. But Jack kept running into the room and screaming for his mother's attention. He was hysterical by now, so we gave up the attempt to hold a conversation. She promised to come down to Money Matters the following morning.

That night in the hotel, I sat down to transcribe the tape of my conversation with Marie. I listened to the thin, beaten voice, the child's screaming interjections, and I knew in my heart Marie would not be coming to Money Matters in the morning. She'd said 'yes' to get rid of me. The 'yes' she used for people who asked anything of her these days. Anything to get them out of her head for a few hours.

I waited at Money Matters but she never came. At three o'clock I drove up to the school: there was no sign of Marie or her younger son. Walking up Drumoyne towards her house, I noticed the digger had finished its work across the road. Any day now the foundations would go down for the new houses. I rang on the buzzer, but there was no answer. A neighbour happened to be on the way out and he left the door open for me. I knocked on the door of the flat and waited. After five minutes I started to scribble a note. The door suddenly opened. Marie was standing inside. She jumped back in fright when she saw me. 'Oh ye bandit!' she shouted. 'I can't talk now, Fergal. I can't see you now,' she said. I backed away and told her not to worry. We could talk another time. Marie was shaking. The little boy was hiding behind her legs. Clothes were strewn across the hallway. I left her my phone number and went away.

Back in Money Matters, I told Geraldine about the encounter. She said she'd go round to try to find out who or what Marie was afraid of. Weeks later somebody else, a neighbour, told me Marie was in a bad way. Her nerves had started to go and she'd thrown the kids out of the house. 'She was afraid of what she might do. That's why she told them to go. She knew one of the neighbours would see them right.' The kids eventually returned home. But their mother was now in serious trouble with another moneylender. The lender had advanced her £400 and was looking for his money. And so Marie had gone into hiding. I called her a few times but her mobile phone was switched off. Geraldine was sure she would turn up at Money Matters, one day or another.

# 3. The Fight of Their Lives

I went back to see Jamie Webster in late spring. By then talks were actively underway to find a buyer for the yard. There were rumours of interest from Swan Hunter and GEC Marconi, but it was all very tentative. And if they did buy, how many men would they keep on? Even if the yard was saved, a lot of people could still end up walking.

You couldn't have told that from the look on Jamie's face. He came hurrying across the yard with a broad smile. I remembered a line of Tom Wolfe's in which a mythical bodyguard is described thus: 'He wasn't a human being, he was a force of nature.' That was Jamie Webster, a force that needed to be stronger than all the fear and uncertainty that sat on the shoulders of men who feared their working life was ending. 'I never give up hope, Fergal. You know that by now. There are talks going on. It can be done.' I nodded and smiled and didn't really believe him. History and the economics of scale seemed set against them. I followed Jamie into the canteen, where 800 men in overalls and hard hats had gathered to hear the latest news about their jobs. There were shouts and jokes. Several men called out Jamie's name, and he smiled at them and gave a thumbs-up sign. Right at that moment he had no solid grounds for optimism, but you'd never have guessed it from the way he addressed those men. 'We can do it. We will do it. I have faith in you.' He told them about the upcoming May Day parade and how the yard men were being given pride of place. 'I want as many of ye there as possible. Show them how much we care about saving this yard.' He looked deep into the crowd, into the faces of men he'd known all his life, who trusted him because he'd never lied to them.

Jamie's trade unionism was about rights and conditions and saving jobs. And if he could help it, no politician would use the men of Govan as a political weapon. This was the yard that had once echoed to the tones of the militant left. There were some of the men who felt Jamie was too much of a moderate, but then he'd never pretended to be anything else. 'Moderate' was the worst thing you would ever hear in the yard about Jamie Webster. I spoke to many men at different times over a year, and not one of them badmouthed their convener. One of the older workers, a man who'd come originally from the Western Isles, told me he'd seen plenty of men with big mouths 'who never achieved a fucking thing except leave workers worse off than they were before'. Jamie wasn't like that.

I had a fair idea of what he meant. My mother lived across the river from a shipyard, the one and only yard in the south of Ireland. The Verolme Cork Dockyard was tiny by the standards of the Clyde. In all eleven hundred men worked there, building ships and refurbishing the coasters which carried cargo around the Irish coast. By the time it closed in 1984 the workforce had shrunk to 410. Industrial relations were appalling and when competition from the Far East began to bite the yard was unable to compete. The yard ended up being totally dependent on the state for work. Since the mid seventies it had failed to win a contract on the open market. There were repeated strikes. In the end the yard closed amid bitter recrimination. I can remember waiting to get the bus to town and looking across at the empty yard. The men were gone and wouldn't be coming back. After a few weeks people along the harbour got used to that emptiness. The cranes and the sheds were still there, and the radio news told us that 'efforts were being made' to get the yard opened again as a going concern. A lot of the men ended up on the dole queues of a city that was already reeling from the closures of the Ford Motor works and the Dunlop Tyre factory. One of my abiding memories of those years is the sight of unemployed men pushing young children around town in buggies or hanging around street corners in town, sitting outside the city library with all the time in the world to do nothing in.

The men in Kvaerner had seen much worse than that. An industry had been dying around them for years. They knew the days of the big strikes and militancy were gone. Some of the men liked to curse Margaret Thatcher as a union breaker. But militancy had vanished in the yard before Thatcher came to power. A century-old decline in shipbuilding – alleviated by big orders in the war years – had undermined the militants, who for years had controlled the Clydeside unions. Thatcher's anti-union policies had far less effect on the Clyde, if only because the power of the unions had already declined in the yards by the time she arrived. In fact it was not the Iron Lady's union policies that had affected the shipyard workers' lives as much as the Tory crusade to create a nation of homeowners. That had completely changed the game, according to Jamie. 'It changed everyone. Once you get a mortgage it changes your concepts. That mortgage has to get paid. The days of having money for drinking pints at lunchtime are gone. You're careful. Your job is all important. You don't want to become unemployed. Thirty years ago maybe 5 per cent of the lads in here had mortgages. Now it's 60 to 70 per cent. Probably 90 per cent among the younger people. It's made them a lot more cautious about industrial disputes.

When you are thinking of a strike, you have to remember there are two people in that house with you. It's not like the old days with the man as the head of the house. Nowadays your wife has just as much say. The fact is most women here control the purse strings. If you go on to hard times and the money is short, the woman is going to have to make it stretch further.'

Jamie Webster had two children at university. His son Fraser was completing a history degree and had been accepted into Sandhurst. If ever you wanted a sign of a changing Britain, that was it: the son of a union convener from Govan becoming an army officer. Men from the yard had served in two world wars, but always as the followers, not givers, of orders. Jamie's youngest daughter, Amanda, was preparing to be a teacher. She was helping to put herself through college by working part time in a local shop. As Jamie himself pointed out, fifty years ago she would have been looking for work in an east end factory or keeping house while her man worked on the Clyde. And there were lots more men in the yard with children either already in college or preparing to go. When you took it all together – the mortgages, the children at college, the dearth of similar work along the Clyde – the pressure to keep the yard open was monumental.

I met Jamie's deputy in the convener's office on the day of the big meeting. Office is an overstatement. It was more a grimy alcove, crammed with filing cabinets and papers and safety notices. There was a kettle just coming to the boil and next to it sat a large man who introduced himself as John Brown. John had short brown hair and a broad expressive face; where Jamie's face could hide feelings, John's was incapable of concealment. They were good friends and he was Jamie's deputy, but temperamentally they were poles apart. When John spoke about the threat to the yard there was an anger and pain you never encountered with Jamie. Not that Jamie wasn't capable of being angry, but in his case it was a professional anger, focused precisely on the task in hand. It went away once the immediate crisis was dealt with. With John it was a long, slow burn. One of the first things he did was to lay into me about the dumbing down of television. He was in the middle of making me a cup of tea when he launched into a detailed critique of the BBC's factual output. That was followed up with a tirade against the historian Simon Schama. He was a committed socialist and a member of the Socialist Workers' Party. When we talked about the yard, he would invariably widen the discussion into the need for all workers to 'come together'. Afterwards, I asked Jamie about his deputy. 'Is that guy the genuine article? All that workers of the world united stuff, is it for real?' 'Oh, aye,' he replied. 'John is the best you could meet. He's a great man to have by your side. He is true to his beliefs.' In time, I would come to the same conclusion myself. But it wasn't until two months later, as the yard looked to be on its last legs, with negotiations going nowhere and the Norwegians set on closure, that I managed to see John on his own. I'd heard from another worker that he was very worried and had put his house on the market. A member of the Socialist Workers' Party he might have been, but John was among the stakeholders in the yard. If he was going to lose his job, then he and his wife and two little boys needed somewhere cheaper to live. From the look on John's face I sensed things were going badly. He made some tea and told me what was happening. 'I'm frightened, Fergal. I just don't know how this thing's goin' to end. I've seen men who lose their jobs, what it does to them. I've seen it tear the fucking heart out of men. I can't afford to sit around and wait for the axe to fall, I've got to start doing something about it now.'

The 'something' he spoke about was selling his house. John's wife was a teacher, but her salary was small. Of the £200 a week he earned, almost three quarters went on childcare fees. If the yard went belly up, then he might have to move to Newcastle or Barrow-in-Furness for work. There were other men talking of going to Holland, where the shipping trade wasn't in the same dire straits. John Brown didn't want to leave Glasgow and his wife and two small boys. The pressure over the future of the yard was causing trouble at home; John said his wife was more militant than him. She was a confident type of person. 'She says to me the other night: "John, you always look at the world as if your glass is half empty, I look at the world as if the glass is half full." And I says to her: "That's because you have choices. You have an education. You have choices. All I can do is labour."' John Brown's father had given his life to the yards. He went to work at the age of fourteen, two years earlier than his son; his mother had worked in Wolsey's tobacco factory in Glasgow's east end. Both parents had to retire early because of bad health. Long days, hard work; bad housing, bad health.

'I didn't have an education. I was bred for factory work. In my class four out of forty went to university. They streamed us; they looked at us and made a value judgement. We were given *Kes* as our textbook, the others got Shakespeare. That was the way it was through school.' There were times when I'd been wary of asking John what he felt about what was happening to him. I feared a tirade against the injustice of the world, topped off with a ringing appeal for class struggle. But when I finally sat down and listened to the story of his life, when I set my own preconceptions to one side, he opened himself up.

John Brown hadn't just been streamed into the weakest class: he was singled out as the weakest of the weak. He found reading difficult: the words jumbled and confused, a tangle of missed connections that left him speechless before the simplest sentences. 'I used to have to sit at the top of the class beside the teacher with all the other kids behind me. They might as well have put a dunce's cap on my head. They didn't click that I was dyslexic until three months before I left school. You were open for ridicule constantly by your classmates. You were the dummy in the class. It doesn't leave a nice taste in your mouth.'

It was hard to set that image – the ten-year-old, humiliated and small before the class – against the John Brown who would happily debate the strategies of Stalin's generals in the Second World War, or give you an erudite assessment of Mao's place among the tyrants of the twentieth century. What pulled him through, he said, was the support and love of two strong parents; they were both of them communists, his father a Christian as well. When he came home from the shame of the classroom, they would sit him down and tell him he was as good as anybody. With professional help he conquered the dyslexia and became a voracious reader. His big hope was to go to university some day. Part of me wanted to say to him that he was made for better things than slogging his guts out for £200 a week in a dying shipyard. I'm glad I didn't. Even if he didn't want his boys to work in the yard, John Brown really believed in the dignity of his own work. What hurt him, still, was the past, how it had diminished him in the eyes of others. In a way, the battle to save the yard was the fight John Brown had spent his life waiting for. The underdogs turning and standing up against those who would deny them a working life. 'I will never be broken. We have to stand together as workers and oppose this,' he told me.

I admit I mentally switched off when John got into his stride on the subject of class struggle. What I would only understand much later was how great a struggle raged inside the man: between the passionate advocate of a workers' struggle, and the man burdened by the need to keep the promise he'd made to himself about his children.

Months after it was all over, a package arrived from Glasgow. Inside was a letter from Jamie Webster and a thick sheaf of pages in the same handwriting. 'Please accept my apologies for the notes being scribbled. I am sure you will be able to decipher them. They might be of some use when you sit down to make sense of it all,' he wrote. I'd been back a few times at key moments and stayed in touch with Jamie by telephone. I'd also read the newspaper accounts of what had happened to the Govan workers. But these were pages from Jamie's personal diary, and they told a story about men and their work you would never have grasped from the facts as disclosed in the public media.

On 5 February 1999 Jamie records: 'My worst fears are confirmed. The directors inform us we have lost the contract. This is a grim situation. I go home for weekend depressed. I also now realize we need to mount a major political, media and public campaign if we are to save the yard and our jobs. The Scottish Office have been told the news and a meeting arranged . . . with Lord Macdonald.'

To the men in the shipyard, the 'Lord', one of Tony Blair's closest political confidants, was plain Gus Macdonald. He was immensely popular and known to be a firm supporter of the campaign. Gus Macdonald had a history in that yard. It was where he'd served his apprenticeship as a fitter. Throughout the diary Macdonald's name crops up as a powerful force of reassurance.

Not every Scottish politician was so well regarded. From early days Jamie and John Brown and the rest of the conveners decided to pursue an independent course: they would liaise with the union head office, but they wouldn't be told what to do. Nor would the Labour Party or the Scottish Nationalists be allowed to make a political football out of the yard. They would all be used, as Jamie said: 'They're accountable. We elected them. Just as I'm accountable to the men, those politicians are accountable to us.' A day before he was due to meet Gus Macdonald, Jamie released the names of fourteen MPs who'd failed to reply to letters from the union conveners. They were all Labour MPs. The release of the names to the press caused uproar. Union head office and Delta House, the HQ of the Labour Party in Scotland, were on the phone complaining. By the end of the day Jamie had earned himself a reputation as a dangerous radical with the union top brass. None of it mattered a damn to him. Politeness and political sensitivity wouldn't count for much if the yard went to the wall.

All the way through, Jamie told the men they'd get a deal. He always insisted to me that he really believed what he was saying. Part of the campaign involved lobbying politicians and management in London. The yard men hated going to London. It was dodgy territory. Politicians and spin doctors and smooth-tongued union bosses abounded. You might come out of the yard with the solid support of 1,200 people, but somewhere in the skies over Britain the nervous trembling in the stomach would get going. The pattern was always the same. Down to the Scottish Office for a make or break meeting with the politicians, Kvaerner and the union

leadership. The media waiting outside and Jamie swamped
with cameras and questions as he went in and out. Afterwards
to the pub for a few pints and a strategy discussion. And then
back to Glasgow to get ready for the mass meeting with the
men the following morning.

By early May there were ominous noises coming from
Kvaerner. The men's hopes should not be raised, the chief
executive said. He was not optimistic that a deal could be
struck. But behind the scenes things were moving. The giant
General Electric Corporation were interested in buying the
yard. I was in the yard chatting with Jamie one day when
he pointed to a group of suits walking around in hard hats.
'They're the GEC men now. Being shown around the
place. I've got to meet them later.'

When he did meet them, Jamie was the picture of moderation. The workers would do everything they could to
make a takeover work. In other words, as long as the
new owners played fair and didn't introduce wholesale
redundancies or seek wage reductions, there wouldn't be
any industrial relations problem. The men were naturally
anxious for news. All Jamie kept repeating was 'Be positive,
I'm sure a deal will be done in about two weeks.' He became
known as 'Jamie Two Weeks'. Paddy Ashdown came. So
did Alex Salmond. With a new, devolved administration in
Scotland, the yard assumed a crucial political importance.
Now Gus Macdonald, the armed forces minister, John
Reid, and Scotland's first minister, Donald Dewar, were all
members of a task force fighting to save the 1,200 jobs.

The Norwegians had set a deadline for a takeover deal. If
the yard hadn't been sold by 16 July, it would be closed.
But by the middle of June, for all the positive talk of a GEC
buyout, there was no deal. News had come through that

GEC was itself being bought by British Aerospace, but that deal was being examined by the Monopolies Commission. If they said no, then the Govan buyout was a non-starter. And Jamie also suspected that the negotiations between GEC and the Norwegians had run into trouble. The companies were arguing over terms. As summer got underway, Jamie's relentless optimism was starting to falter. In his diary for 15 June 1999, he wrote: 'Mass meeting of workforce with update. Again I emphasize resiliance, patience and unity . . . for the first time I detect an edginess and a degree of frustration coming across. I'm not surprised. I feel the same way but I *must* emit positivity.'

One of those feeling edgy was John Brown. It was starting to look likely that even if there was a takeover, significant redundancies were possible. With his reputation as one of the more militant union figures, John felt sure his name would be on any list drawn up by the new owners. On the day the GEC men came into the yard, John watched them warily, sizing up his own chances of survival. John had plenty of friends who were doing the rounds of Call Centres and Programme Centres. 'I've seen what that does to men. It tears them in half, it does. I was not made for standin' in a queue with some wee lassie at the top treatin' me like I was nothin'. That stuff really changes you, knocks the purpose out a' ye.' There was no sign yet of his house selling. It had been on the market for four months without even an offer. And so he was asking himself, every night, *What will we do if the job goes and I haven't sold the house? How will we pay the mortgage?* And after that came the bigger questions about his own life, what would happen to him if he had nothing to do all day but wander the city looking for jobs that weren't there.

With two weeks to go before the deadline there was still

no official bid for the yard. 'What the hell is going on?' wrote Jamie in his diary. For the first time men were coming up to him and starting to commiserate in advance. If there wasn't a deal it wouldn't be his fault. It wouldn't be for want of trying. On 2 July 1999 he wrote: 'They think it'll make me feel the pressure less saying that. It does not.'

Three days later the management of Kvaerner told Jamie they would be sending out letters to all employees, seeking volunteers for redundancy. The union immediately decided to ask the men not to volunteer. Nobody should respond, instead the conveners would take all the unopened letters to Kvaerner's head office in London. A worker on the shopfloor came up with that one.

That night Jamie was sitting down to his tea when the phone rang. It was BBC Radio Clyde to tell him an announcement about a deal was imminent. Immediately he went off to the studio with his daughter Amanda.

The official GEC statement came through as Jamie was waiting outside the studio. 'GEC have today tabled a bid for the purchase of the yard which they feel will form the basis of an agreement.'

'Ecstasy! Total joy! I am overcome with emotion,' Jamie recorded in his diary.

On the way home in the taxi Amanda tried to inject a note of caution. It was only an offer, she said, no *deal* had been announced. Jamie was having none of that. There were only technicalities to be sorted out.

When he got home his wife, Isabel, said there were twenty-five phone calls waiting to be answered. Most were from the media, anxious for his comments on the forth-coming deal. After the fourth conversation, he paused for a moment, and the phone rang with an incoming call. It was the Press Association in London.

'Hello, Jamie, it's Richard. Have you heard the news?'

'Yes, Richard. I'm totally ecstatic.'

'Jamie, have you heard the *latest* news?'

'What do you mean?'

'Jamie, Kvaerner have rejected the deal.'

Jamie went quiet. The man on the other end apologized for being the bearer of bad news. Jamie started to feel physically sick. As he was sitting there, his mobile phone went: a Labour MP wanting to congratulate him on the deal. Jamie couldn't answer, so his wife passed on the latest news. In the space of an hour 1,200 jobs went from being saved to being lost. Jamie left the house and took a walk. He was thinking of the men and their families listening to the radio. How they must have jumped up and shouted when the GEC bid was announced. And then to hear that it wasn't going to happen after all. For the first time he had to contemplate standing in front of a mass meeting while he told them they were losing the battle.

Jamie didn't sleep that night. He was still supposed to go to London the following morning with the box full of unopened redundancy letters, the men's statement of faith in the future of the yard. The arrangement was that the men would leave their letters at the gatehouse for Jamie to collect. But after this? Wouldn't they just want to look for redundancy packages and get out? Jamie arrived at the yard early and walked up to the gatehouse. His heart was pounding and his throat dry.

'Did the nightshift leave their notices?' he asked the guard.

'Oh aye, Jamie. They're all in boxes, every one of them,' he replied.

Men from the dayshift were arriving at the same time. They walked up and started handing over their notices to

Jamie and wishing him 'good luck' in London. Tears came to his eyes. Before he headed for London he did a series of interviews, telling the media that Tony Blair should make a statement in the Commons. Later that day the Prime Minister praised the 'commitment and passion' of the Clyde workers.

Down in London, Jamie and his colleagues handed over the unopened redundancy offers and headed into another meeting with Kvaerner. The message from the Norwegians was straightforward: the unions would have to pressurize the politicians, so that they in turn pressurized GEC into making a deal. If they could do that, then Kvaerner would move as well. Afterwards the union men met Gus Macdonald and other senior Labour politicians and passed on the message: it was time to really press GEC.

There was now just one week to the deadline. At a mass meeting in the yard the following day, Jamie stood up and told the workers yet again that a deal could be done. He had in his mind something the armed forces minister, John Reid, had said to him the previous day. 'Jamie, last week in London with Gus Macdonald we gave you an assurance we'd bust a gut to get a deal. That promise is still on the table.'

Jamie believed him, but by 13 July no deal had been done and management said they'd be issuing compulsory redundancy notices to 241 men – the beginning of the end. The atmosphere in the yard was worsening. That afternoon the supervisors went around handing out the redundancy notices to the selected men. John Brown was among those given a letter telling him his working life in the yard was over. Somebody who met him that afternoon said he was shell-shocked, just sitting there in the small office, wondering what he was going to do with the rest of his life. Jamie was telling everybody to stay calm. John Brown was pitching between anger and panic.

That night John went home and broke the news to his wife. She took it in her stride. They would be all right. At least she had a job. John would be able to find work somehow, and if that didn't happen he could always try to get a grant to study. Maybe he could mind the kids and study part time.

In Jamie's kitchen, Isabel was telling him he'd done his best. If it all went wrong, he wasn't to blame himself. And then at around half past seven the phone rang. It was the Press Association from London. There was a deal. A genuine, cast-iron agreement. There would be ninety-seven redundancies but the majority would be voluntary. The threat of mass lay-offs was gone. 'Absolute joy, what a happy house!' noted Jamie in his diary.

When John Brown got the news from the radio later that evening, he sat down in his kitchen and wondered what to feel. His name was on a list of ninety-seven men who would be made redundant. All the fear and frustration of that fighting year coursed through him as he tried to reconcile his happiness for the other men with the fear about his own future.

He was in the yard a few days later, when the supervisor came up with some good news. Another man had volunteered to take redundancy in his place – his job was saved. Though he knew he should feel happy and grateful, John felt empty and exhausted.

The Kvaerner yard and the jobs of 1,200 men were sold for two and a quarter million pounds. It was the kind of money you would pay for a big house in a fashionable part of London. The following day Jamie was driving down the Govan Road, that broken spine of a community along which defeated men had been tramping in retreat for decades, when he noticed something different about the figures walking in the midsummer morning. 'You could see from the way they were walking, from their body language. It was a confident walk,' he said. And then he mimicked the march of the undefeated men of Kvaerner, heading for the jobs they'd saved. 'There were guys coming up all morning saying "Well done, Jamie", and I said to them: "Savour this day, lads. We've done something incredible. Don't feel arrogant but do feel proud." It was the kind of feeling that engulfs you when your kid is born. You know, there was a boy in here who won the lottery and I said to him he couldn't have been as happy as I was when I knew the deal was signed. And he said back to me: "You're right, Jamie. You are right."'

The men of Govan took control of their lives. And they took control of the political agenda in a way that people like them hadn't managed to do for decades. They did it without strikes or sit-ins. They kept doing their jobs, they showed potential buyers that this was a workforce committed to making the yard a viable enterprise again. They pressurized politicians relentlessly, they used the media as a weapon to shame, embarrass and flatter. They took a simple proposition – that people had a right to the dignity of work – and they never let go of it. Certainly they were lucky that the fight was being waged at a time when the political parties were trying to maximize their support in the new Scottish Assembly. And they had good friends in men like their old workmate Gus Macdonald. But the victory belonged to the workers in the end. Everybody knew that. They had looked long enough at the world beyond the gates, and promised themselves they wouldn't easily submit to the slow death of joblessness.

★

I returned to Glasgow to see Jamie and John in the last month of the old century. Jamie was his usual, energetic self. The yard was in the running for new M.o.D. contracts. If they landed those, the future was secure. GEC had warned that there were no absolute guarantees: everything depended on getting new contracts. 'I'm out of here in fifteen years, and the day I walk out I want to see a bunch of apprentices passing me on the way in. That for me will be the measure of whether we really succeeded or not.'

And then he told me that John Brown had quit his union post. John, who'd been the most angry and passionate of all the shop stewards, had volunteered for the nightshift. Why, I wanted to know.

'Ye better ask him yourself,' Jamie said.

I met John as he was clocking out. I was glad to see him. It wasn't just the fact of enjoying his intelligence, or the arguments about politics. There was a great sincerity and a great gentleness about him.

I asked him whether it was true that he'd quit his union job.

'It's true,' he said.

It was nothing to do with wanting a lower profile. Nothing at all to do with wanting to keep out of the way of management. It was just down to economics and childcare. If he worked the nightshift, starting at half past eleven, he earned extra shift allowances, and he got to see his boys a lot more. He worked while they were asleep. It meant he was around in the day to take them to nursery and collect them. 'I've not been broken by this, Fergal. I'll never be broken,' he said.

# 4. Submerged

*One hundred and eighty dead.* I heard the news on the radio the morning I left Glasgow. *One hundred and eighty dead in Strathclyde.* In just one county council area of the United Kingdom, that was the total number of deaths from heroin overdose in the last year of the twentieth century. One of the dead was a Scottish government minister's son. The street word was that a lot of those who'd overdosed had mixed their heroin with the sleeping tablet temazepam. It made the smack go a lot further. But one hundred and eighty dead? It was more people than had died in the last four years of the Northern Ireland Troubles. The government told us it was at war with drugs. And down on the streets of Strathclyde, Liverpool, Manchester, London, Leeds, the casualties were mounting.

I have a friend who fights in the government's 'war' on drugs. Every so often, when he comes to dinner with his wife, I ask him how the war is going. He is one of nature's realists. The war can't be won on the streets of Britain, he says. We'll only turn the tide by getting the producers at source. Nail the Colombian, Afghan, Iranian and Turkish drug gangs. But what about the dead here? Why were we losing so many people? My friend put it down to economics. Heroin had never been cheaper. The £20 bag was now the £10 bag: the same score but at half the price. Even the government's drug czar, Keith Halliwell, spoke of kids being able to buy 'hits' at £2 a go. Up on the plains of Afghanistan, the poppy fields were yielding record crops. The best in years. And with the help of God knows how many private armies and gangsters, the heroin was flowing over the mountains, up through Iran and Turkey and across Europe to Britain. The laws of supply and demand had brought the price crashing down, and the streets of the United Kingdom were awash with the stuff. My friend was probably right about the big picture. The police could be raiding houses until doomsday, but new dealers would keep springing up. For in Britain at the close of the twentieth century there was no end of a market for the self-obliterating remedy of heroin. The figures released by the National Statistics Office for the last years of the millennium showed that one fifth of all deaths among men in their twenties were caused by drugs. Between 1993 and 1997 the estimated number of deaths from heroin per year had jumped from 67 to 255. And even that, the government agreed, was definitely an underestimate.

If you'd walked the streets of Leeds, the fastest-growing city of the north, in the last few months of 1999, it would have been hard not to notice the beggars who hovered in doorways or wandered up and down Briggate rattling coins in McDonald's paper cups. Some of them sold the *Big Issue* and others just begged. The ones too stoned or strung out to do either just stumbled from one street corner to the next. You couldn't miss them. The taxi driver who picked me up from Leeds Station figured all the down and out young people in the north had heard about the boom times and descended on the city. It was the biggest free lunch in the north, he said. And be assured, Leeds *was* thriving. It had the second-lowest unemployment total of any city in the UK. In the early nineties it had managed to mark a rise in real estate values when prices all over the north were falling. There was money in the air. You could sense it walking up Briggate, the commercial heart of the city, looking at the sun glint on the plate-glass windows of Harvey Nichols, listening to the shoppers as they paused over coffee in Costa Coffee or Starbucks.

The central shopping area had been pedestrianized. The shoppers loved it and so did the beggars. Neither had to worry about the inhibiting dangers of traffic. Nor, it must be said, did the people with money express any obvious hostility towards those who had none. It was not like London, where the free-falling teenagers and destitute older men and women strained to puncture the thousand-yard stare of the daily commuter. They were a nuisance whom we wished invisible. But in Leeds there were still plenty of people who stopped to give money to the homeless and to talk with them.

Most of the beggars I saw in Leeds were in their late teens or early twenties. I never met one who wasn't willing to talk. Naturally most wanted to know if you were drug squad or social welfare, but once satisfied that your inquiries would bring no sanction on their heads, they opened up. Certainly not all, probably not even the majority, of the beggars were drug addicts. But once you asked around, spoke with people, the drugs crisis the media talked about took on living form. These were invariably snatched conversations, mumbled out of the haze of a high or muttered through the desperation of the penniless dawn hours before the shoppers arrived.

A few names and short stories: the boy 'Francis', whose teeth were rotting and who smelled of old shit and sweat. He had long, shaggy, fair hair that hung over his eyes and which he would flick back over his head every few seconds. The blackened shards of his teeth showed every time he opened his mouth. Francis was about nineteen or twenty, though his precise age, like everything else in his life, was something about which he found it difficult to be certain. One of his mates who shared a room with him said Francis was sick with hepatitis B, an occupational hazard among the drug users of Britain's streets. His mother was a junkie, and she'd introduced him to heroin at the age of fifteen. He'd been living with his mother's problem for years. All the lying and abandonment of active addiction had been his birthright from early days. Then she'd taken him on the last stage of the journey, handing him the needle, the gear and the longing. A year after that she dumped him and his brother, leaving them in a graveyard. I only met him twice, and there was never time to get into the business of the graveyard. He could not or would not tell me why she'd left them there, of all places. He lived in the grave-yard for months before linking up with some other junkies. And now he begged on the streets of central Leeds. Francis was well down the road of addiction. He never stopped to talk for long, always on the move, hustling for the £10 bag.

Up the street there was 'Jimmy', who sold the *Big Issue* and was trying to kick smack. If you didn't know his story, you would have assumed Jimmy was a very regular guy who'd just hit a rough patch. His clothes were always immaculate, and he wore his hair cut short and neat. Jimmy was as far from the conventional image of the street junkie as you could imagine. He claimed he had himself down to one bag a day. He had promised his parents in Halifax that he'd be off the stuff by New Year's Eve. It was going to be their millennium present. Jimmy had lost his job with a transport firm due to his habit of disappearing for hours on end to find gear. But his father said there was a chance he'd get the old job back if he cleaned up his act. And now he was selling lots of copies of the *Big Issue* with plenty of regular customers. I watched him in action and marvelled at his charm. People would cross the street to buy his magazines. They would stand talking with him for ten or fifteen minutes. It was late autumn, and Jimmy had two months left to go before his deadline. When I looked for him not long before Christmas, he wasn't standing at his normal pitch. Perhaps he had gone home or taken the day off. I never found out whether he met the deadline.

The addicts among the beggars all seemed to know each other. When Francis vanished, I asked one of his friends what had happened. 'He's in jail. They've done him for possession. The best fucking place for him. At least they'll feed him.'

Leeds didn't have the worst drug problem in the United Kingdom. You could find estates in Liverpool or London that would make the Leeds problem look modest. What initially drew me to Leeds wasn't even the drugs crisis per se, it was a story of sadistic cruelty as bad as any I'd covered in a foreign country. I'd heard about the murder on the radio, a killing on a Leeds council estate that was reported towards the end of the bulletin. The killing had been carried out by a gang of young people, five of them aged between seventeen and twenty-two, who were using an empty flat near the city centre as a squat. Their victim was Angela Pearce, an eighteen-year-old woman with a history of mental illness. Doctors had diagnosed Angela as schizophrenic. She was not a tough child. The newspaper photograph shows a blonde, smiling girl. She looks happy and – there isn't another word for it – innocent. Angela wanted to belong, and that most basic of human needs brought her into the company of a group of young people who would become her murderers.

According to the courtroom account of what happened, Angela was lured by a group of teenage girls to an empty flat in a tower block about ten minutes' walk from the city centre. Back at the flat, the girls were joined by a couple of boys. They decided to have some fun with Angela. They started out by beating her up. A seventeen-year-old girl is described as having kicked and hit Angela several times. They burned her face with cigarettes. A witness said her eyes were swollen to the size of tennis balls. When she asked for a drink of water, they gave her disinfectant. The witness said they laughed at her when she cried out. They forced her to lie down behind the settee and turned up the music whenever anybody came to visit. This was to drown out her cries. Eventually they suffocated her with a plastic bag. The body was wrapped in a blanket and taken out into the snow. The gang dug a shallow grave in a disused cemetery near by and buried Angela Pearce. Over six days these young citizens tortured the life out of a vulnerable eighteen-year-old. The court report was horrible enough. But no dispassionate rendering of the evidence can do justice to the human truth of murder, especially a prolonged agony like that experienced by Angela. Nobody heard her cries of pain, or, if they did, they didn't come to her aid or call the police. This did not happen in a lonely cottage on the moors, but in a flat surrounded by other flats on a city council estate.

I had seen a lot of torture and murder in the ten years prior to my coming to live in Britain. Much of it involved pain inflicted on children in times of war. Opposing armies murdering whole families. Rwandan genocidaire smashing kids' heads against walls. Schoolgirls raped by marauding gangs in Soweto. But all of that had taken place in societies convulsed by political unrest. It was savage and at times surreal, but I could explain it to myself, there was a political context into which the horror could be placed. Even in Northern Ireland, where the pain was happening to people you knew, or where your drive into work might take you past a club in which somebody had been tortured and beaten to death, even there you could find in the three hundred years of history a general statement of explanation. But the country in which I had now come to live, the country of Angela Pearce's murder, was not at war. It was a peaceful, democratic state that had only recently elected a new government on a wave of hope and prosperity.

What was going on here? How did these young people sink into the place where slow torture and murder became their response to the weakness and *otherness* of Angela Pearce? Later I would come to believe that the Angela Pearce case was but one of many red flashing lights. I only paid attention to it then because the facts of the case struck me as a horrible anachronism in Tony Blair's new Britain. The defence lawyer spoke of Leeds as a city with a twin-track economy. The killers, he implied, had come from the wrong side of the tracks. To the casual observer, they seemed to live outside the boundaries of new Britain; they seemed impervious to the ordinary claims of human kindness, much less to the notion of a reborn community trumpeted in the heady days of May 1997. The defence lawyer was right: the Pearce killing happened in another city. It was not the Leeds of Harvey Nichols or Marks & Spencer or Costa Coffee, but a city of high-rise flats and dreary estates into which human lives could disappear and be nullified.

Though this chapter is not the story of Angela Pearce, hers was the name that drew me to Lincoln Green in the first place. It was she who gave human substance to the relentlessly repeated idea of a crisis on the margins of British society. For a few weeks in a Leeds courtroom the story of her life and death illuminated a parallel universe in which young men, women and children lived not so much on the wrong side of the tracks, but far below the surface of the nation. *Submerged*. The majority did not end up killing or engaging in senseless violence, nor could they in any sense be said to inhabit the same moral universe as those who murdered Angela Pearce.

But they did live in the submerged world. It was there all around us, in every city in the country, a world of unexplained departures and missed connections, a great, quiet tragedy that went stalking down the generations. When it spilled on to our front pages – a child dead from neglect or cruelty, a frightening drug statistic – we took notice, we were shocked. But the waves always closed over and the underwater silence resumed.

The addicts begging in central Leeds whom I'd met were by no means hard core. They generally found their fix-money within the confines of the law. Maybe some graduated to stealing later on and maybe a few of them managed to quit using. But those I call the submerged . . . the newcomer could find it hard to spot them. They didn't cluster outside in gangs or otherwise go out of their way to advertise their presence.

The journey in search of their voices began with a brisk walk from Briggate through the markets area and across the ring road. Standing at the traffic lights, I could see straight ahead on a hill the building that locals called the 'Kremlin', a huge lump of red brick with a steel turret that dominated the skyline for miles around. The Kremlin was the head-quarters of the Department of Social Security. Pushing up the hill, I walked past the Leeds Playhouse – latest attraction, a hugely popular production of *Macbeth* – and up several sets of steps towards the motorway. Through the roar of the traffic I could hear shouting. I looked around and couldn't see another soul. The voices were those of children, laughing and swearing. I scanned the bridge over the motorway and spotted two small figures, boys of roughly ten years of age, sliding down the concrete incline about twenty feet above the road. A slip or fall would have carried them directly into the path of the traffic below. They noticed me looking at them and started to dance. The words 'fucking' and 'tosser' sailed on reedy voices over the noise of the traffic. This was eleven o'clock in the morning on a school day.

On the other side of the motorway, the road sloped upwards in the direction of the Lincoln Green Estate. There were thirteen high-rise towers, each perched on a patch of green open ground. Spread out around them were several rows of small houses and maisonettes. The first set of houses I passed was neat and well maintained. Some had flowers planted in their tiny gardens, all had the look of places whose owners felt a pride in their appearance. These were houses that had been bought from the council. At the heart of the estate was a shopping centre built around a small square. The square was the focal point of community life on the estate. It contained a fish and chip shop, a pharmacy, a bakery, a supermarket, a newsagent, a launderette and a post office. These last two were perhaps the only places in the centre where the people of Lincoln Green gathered and spoke with one another for any sustained period of time. Forty-six per cent of the population received some kind of benefit from the state, and on Thursday mornings the queue stretched out of the square to the street beyond, as pensioners and young families waited to collect their entitlements.

Four doors up was the launderette run by a formidable grandmother called Doreen Warden and her daughter Jane. They had lived in the area all their lives, initially in the old back-to-back houses on Quarry Hill that had been demolished to make way for the Lincoln Green Estate. Doreen was quick-witted and very funny, with a look of perpetual puzzlement on her face. Her flat was on the other side of the square above the supermarket, about three minutes' walk from work. You might have thought this arrangement ideal. But Doreen hated the estate and pined for her old terraced house up near St James Hospital. Number One Alma Terrace was now a pile of rubble and weeds awaiting development. You could still walk the cobbled streets upon which her children had once played. But the neighbourly world she recalled had vanished with the demolition of the houses.

When I called into the launderette she was sitting chatting with her friend Margaret Rea, a small, bird-like woman who'd been a neighbour in Quarry Hill. Margaret had nine grandchildren and eight great-grandchildren, and said Lincoln Green had gone to hell. Nobody cared about anybody. The old people lived in fear of their lives. It was full of junkies and drunkards. That was progress for you. Doreen agreed, but took the view that she had no choice but to make the best of things. For both of them it was much too late to think of leaving.

Just across the road from the launderette, beside the soon to be demolished Granville Arms, stood a row of derelict maisonettes. They too were due for demolition, and teams of council workers were busy erecting steel hoardings on the windows and doors. The idea was to keep the squatters and junkies out until the council got round to demolishing the flats. The problem for Leeds Council was that Lincoln

Green's reputation as a haven for junkies made it hard to rent flats to any but the most desperate. And this category included a fair proportion of drug abusers and alcoholics.

The council had produced a glossy brochure offering flats for rent at around £33 per week. 'All fully decorated, light, airy one- and two-bedroomed flats,' it declared. There were photographs of neatly maintained and well-furnished apartments. But when you entered those towers, walked past the graffiti-smeared walls, inhaled the urine and disinfectant smell in the lifts, heard the voices of teenagers screaming up and down the shafts, then the prospect of settling down to domestic bliss as suggested in the council brochure became distinctly unattractive. The towers were dank and lonely places, reeking of transience and disappointment. And if you were old in such a place, or a young mother or an unemployed man, the world could close in around you very quickly. In the day-care centre for the elderly on Lincoln Green, there were plenty of old people who could tell you about the shadows that came alive with danger on pension day.

The community policeman Tony Sweeney heard these stories all the time. The old men and women bombarded him with complaints about junkies. And he would dutifully note down what they said and do what he could, which much of the time was very little. Sweeney was the community copper, and he had made the hard-core junkies of Lincoln Green his personal target. He produced a newsletter called *Billy the Burglar* that announced and denounced various crimes in the area, and he remorselessly harried anyone he remotely suspected of dealing in drugs.

Sweeney had grown up in the area, and most of the old people remembered him as a youngster going to the Church of England school up near the main road. When Sweeney left school, there were few jobs around. And so he joined the army and ended up as a sergeant leading platoons of men on the streets of Belfast. Tony Sweeney was a broad-chested, red-headed, plain-speaking soldier who found himself in the frontline of a war against drugs that was killing more people than he'd ever seen lost in the battleground of Ulster. He did his rounds of the area on a bicycle, and, as far as I could gather, he was well respected. Even the junkies I got to know agreed that he was straight and gave you a chance if he thought you were cleaning up.

I was in a flat once with a young couple who were struggling to come down from heroin. They had a baby but neither had a job. Halfway through the conversation Tony Sweeney knocked on the door. A few days beforehand somebody had tried to break into the flat. Sweeney had come to advise them on security. He was genuinely con-cerned for them. But if he suspected you were dealing in smack or were a hard-core user, he made a point of stopping and questioning you every time he crossed your path. He wanted the pushers and the serious users out of Lincoln Green, and if that meant pushing the problem into someone else's district, then so be it. He had a tribal loyalty to his own place and to the people he regarded as 'honest, decent citizens'. This was a definition that excluded the majority of drug users on the estate. If you walked through Lincoln Green with him, people would stop to talk and pass on their complaints about what this or that neighbour was doing. A lot of it was about drunks making noise or dogs left locked up all day and howling every time somebody on the other side of the wall made a move. PC Sweeney always listened and took careful note.

We were sitting outside a block of flats one afternoon when a young black woman approached us. 'That's Mercy now,' said Sweeney, 'she's from Malawi. A lovely young girl. Imagine, she can't get a flat here 'cos she's a foreigner and lowlifes can simply 'cos they're English.' Mercy was a student nurse at St James Hospital up at the top of the estate. For complicated reasons to do with her foreign student status, she said she couldn't get a long-term rental on one of the flats. This, in spite of the fact that the council was desperate to find tenants. Mercy chatted to Sweeney for a few minutes, and he promised to get on to the housing people and do what he could.

If we bumped into somebody he regarded as suspicious, a different Sweeney emerged. It was the soldier doing a p-check in Belfast. Focused and cold.

'Are you from round here?'

'Yeah, I live in the flats.'

'Which one?'

'Eh, back over there in Spalding Towers.'

'How long are you there? I don't know your face.'

'Oh, I'm 'ere a right few months, Tony.'

'Is that right. Who are you living with?'

'Oh, just some of me mates.'

'Do I know any of 'em?'

'Don't know if you do, Tony, do I?'

And on it would go until Sweeney, having registered his presence, would say goodbye and continue his patrol. The man wasn't blind to the causes of crime. He had grown up around poverty and had spent a large part of his life commanding young men who'd escaped the dole queue by joining the army. I sensed he knew that his own campaign made at best a marginal difference. He understood that the big battles belonged to the politicians, that the big solutions had to do with jobs and housing. But he ploughed on, covering the miles back and forth on foot or on his bicycle.

Sweeney had a good intuition about people, and I believed him when he said he could spot a spoofer a long way off. One day he was called to a break-in at a flat in Boston Towers. The complainant was a seventeen-year-old girl who had moved to Lincoln Green because she couldn't get along with her mother. There were two other teenage girls staying with her. She claimed the flat had been broken into the previous night. Sweeney went around and checked the place. The girl said the burglar had broken the bathroom window to get in. But nothing had been taken, and Sweeney didn't believe there had been any break-in.

He took his notes and told the girl to think about reinforcing the window.

'That was probably a boyfriend did that,' he said to me afterwards. 'If she says it was crime, then the council will fix the window. If it was just someone forgot a key, or maybe there was a row and the window got broken, then she'll have to fork out for it herself.'

It was an ordinary occurrence. Sweeney didn't believe the girl was a serious drug addict. More likely she was just enjoying the first joys of freedom after escaping from home. Young she was, but not unwise in the ways of high-rise life.

Once he took me to the flat of a hard-core heroin addict. The tenant had vanished, and now the council wanted to clean the place out. Steel hoardings had been placed over the windows and front door. Sweeney's job, along with a council official, was to record the physical condition of the flat. That way if the tenant reappeared the council could bar him from taking up occupation again. There was a strange, acrid smell to the place, like burned plastic mixed with the rank odour of sweaty bodies. According to Sweeney, the tenant had shared the flat with four or five other addicts. Inside the hallway there was a pile of unopened letters: Telecom, Leeds City Council, the DSS. I spotted a handwritten note among them. It read: 'D–, you owe me fifty quid. I haven't forgotten and I will be coming back, G——.' There were dirty clothes piled everywhere. Inside the bedroom a tattered Union Jack was draped over a chair below a page-three portrait from the *Sun*. A piece of lingerie, a bodice, was stretched across the window and below it lay a pile of condoms. Next to the condoms was a baby's dummy. The bedroom was a model of neatness compared to the sitting room next door.

'Watch your feet,' warned PC Sweeney. I looked down and saw that the carpet was littered with used needles. Scores of them. On the wall were several children's drawings. Sweeney believed there had been kids staying in the flat. I hadn't seen anything like it since entering the abandoned houses of refugees in central Africa. Back then the domestic chaos had been inflicted by looting soldiers. Here in this tiny flat in Lincoln Green I was walking through the debris of long-term addiction. I came back to the word *submerged*. This was a world below the world – to those who lived down there everything was reduced to a simple, self-obliterating quest. Heroin. Golden and calming. The one sure thing, if you could find the money. Tony Sweeney had shown me the world of drugs from his side, that of the frustrated community policeman who saw the junkies as the biggest threat to law and order in Lincoln Green. It was a viewpoint that naturally enough made the addicts disinclined to trust anybody who kept his company. They must have seen me walking around the estate with him and wondered who I was and what I was up to.

I would never have heard the voices or stories of the submerged were it not for a man I will call 'Jacob'. I cannot give his name or describe what he does for a living. To do so would break my word and would shatter the confidence of those he is trying to help. Let's just say he was part psychologist, nurse, activist, dreamer and a whole lot of other things besides. Most of all he was a listener, and he looked out for the ones who were slipping towards the end of their road. If you hung around long enough with Jacob, you learned to spot the look and walk of a long-term addict: the eyes a thousand miles away, the shoulders hunched forward into the wind and the give-away limp. Here was a body that had run out of places to inject. Jacob's people only surfaced to steal and score, and they were adept at vanishing. A flat lived in for months could be vacated in minutes. They owned nothing. They had nothing to pack.

Jacob wasn't a junkie himself, but he liked to drink a lot. I think he knew that if he once picked up heroin, he might never put it down. There was something in him that recognized the emptiness on which addiction feeds. His way out of that was to stay busy and help others. I don't think his motivation was very different from that of Tony Sweeney. They both wanted the despair and anguish caused by heroin to disappear. But Jacob thought you just drove the problem deeper underground by hounding the addicts. And whatever people like him or Tony Sweeney did, the drugs would still be there, flooding in from the Middle East. The fundamental difference was that Jacob believed in controlling the problem; Sweeney believed that with political will and resources it could be destroyed. This man, about whom I must be so vague, understood my need to find those other voices. You could say he regarded it as his moral duty to make sure I did listen to and *hear* their stories. It was through Jacob that I met Fiona Stewart and her boyfriend Kevin who, in the first days of our acquaintance, lived on the fifth floor of Boston Towers. If my journey to

Lincoln Green could be said to have begun with the little newspaper clipping about the murder of Angela Pearce, it ended with the story of Fiona and Kevin.

I never really got to know Kevin. He was always on the move, limping to his falling-asunder car and vanishing whenever I showed up. The limp came from the constant injections of heroin into his groin, while the suspicion of me or any outsider was a matter of instinct. Kevin looked like a hard man. He'd been in jail a few times and was facing another string of drug-related charges. Fiona reckoned he did an average of two months inside every year. Kevin's face was gaunt, framed by lank black hair and prematurely lined. A cigarette dangled permanently from the side of his mouth.

By contrast, Fiona was pretty and petite. She was twenty-five years old with long brown hair and dark brown eyes. Fiona had lost a lot of weight since becoming a heroin addict. Her high cheekbones stood out more than they should have. The last time she weighed herself she was down to six stone. It should have been eight. Before heroin she had been training to work as a beautician. And throughout the time I was in contact with her, she worked hard at keeping up appearances. We met outside Boston Towers, just as she and Kevin were coming home. It was eleven o'clock in the morning and they'd been away for the night. Jacob didn't ask where and they didn't volunteer the information.

Jacob made the introductions. 'He just wants to know what your life is like, you know. What it's like living here and all that.' Kevin didn't stop to talk and walked off in the direction of the lift. Fiona stood for a few moments considering the proposition that somebody would be interested in her life. She was shivering and seemed nervous.

'Sure. That's fine,' she said, 'just give me a few minutes to get myself ready for visitors.' Jacob said he had other people to see and headed off for the morning.

After about ten minutes Kevin came out and told me to go on up to the flat. He got into the car and drove away. Fiona was more relaxed now. The shivering and edginess were gone. There was a faint dreamy undercurrent to her movements and speech. Later I would recognize this as the 'normal' time. It wasn't that she was high – in her own words, just 'normal'. The heroin she'd injected while I was waiting outside did not transport her to paradise. It simply allowed her to function without shivering, sweating and vomiting. Fiona was so deeply into her addiction that it would have taken a lot more than the small amount she'd just injected to make her high.

The flat was dirty and untidy but nothing as bad as the temple of chaos I'd visited a few weeks before with Tony Sweeney. In Fiona's flat there were food stains on the carpet and a pile of dirty duvets behind the couch. Two black kittens chased each other across the floor. 'They're my babies,' said Fiona. On the wall was a photograph of Fiona and Kevin on holiday in Greece. They were in a restaurant, tanned and smiling at the end of a day on the beach. The young woman in the photograph was bright-eyed and a little plump. Kevin too looked much fitter and younger, though the photograph had been taken only a few years before. Altogether, they'd been going out for seven years. Fiona smiled when she remembered the beginning of their courtship. He'd been chasing her for six months after they'd first met up in the Strega Bar in Chapeltown. Kevin was handsome and strong, and he made her laugh. Fiona was already part of the drugs scene by the time she met up with him. All of her mates were doing ecstasy or crack, and one night in a club she'd said yes to crack and hadn't stopped using it since.

Fiona had grown up in a terraced house just down the road from Lincoln Green. When she was four years old her father walked out. She still didn't know why. Nor did she know where he was now. Her mother met and married a man whom Fiona described as 'the nicest man she ever met'. He treated her like his natural daughter. The kind stepfather died of a heart attack on her twenty-first birthday. She remembered sitting on her bed crying as she opened her presents. A few years after that her mother collapsed with a brain haemorrhage. She survived but was left seriously weakened.

Drugs took Fiona out of her beauty therapy course. They took her fast and far. Down to London, where she went on the game to get money for her habit. It wasn't on the streets, she assured me. Men came to her in a house where she worked shifts with other girls. 'After a while you didn't think about it. I made good money. You got your mind to tell you it wasn't you that was there.' She was a weekend prostitute, travelling down from Leeds on the Inter-City Express. However much she must have tried to blank out what was being done to her body, Fiona clearly hated the 'game'. After a few months she stopped going to London and turned to petty crime to pay for her habit. She became a dedicated shoplifter. There were arrests and convictions. She'd spent a week in jail on remand but had escaped a sentence. Gradually she became known to the security guards in every major store in Leeds. These days she spread her net further afield, travelling across Yorkshire to rob for drug money. 'It terrifies me, it does. Every time I'm heading for the door I'm scared shitless.' Fiona dreaded getting sent back to jail. I imagined it was because she was afraid of bullying or abuse. 'No, not that. I've got lots of mates inside. It's the thought of coming down off this stuff cold. It was bloody hell the last time,' she said. 'I'm scared of the pain. Can you understand that? It's the pain that happens if you try to get away from this stuff.'

Fiona did not want me to feel sorry for her. That is a rare enough thing when you are dealing with active addicts. Nor did she want to blame anybody else for her predicament. 'It's nobody's fault but my own,' she would say. Not the fault of her fractured childhood or the grim streets she'd grown up on, not her teachers or the government, and not Kevin, her lover and fellow junkie. He chased the gear with her, he drove her on the stealing missions and in his bad moments he would take his fist to her.

I would never have known that were it not for an incident outside the flat one afternoon. I was standing with the camera team, who were filming Fiona as she walked from one end of her balcony to the other. A man appeared in a doorway halfway along.

'What the fuck is going on?' he shouted.

A wiry, blond-haired figure came out behind Fiona and walked towards us, another of the thin, angry faces that haunted the estate. He was about thirty years old, with a tattoo of a heart pierced by an arrow on his left forearm.

'Here. Who the fuck do you think you are, filming my house, eh?'

The sound recordist tried to tell him what we were doing. He wasn't in the mood to listen. 'Hey, four eyes, shut your fucking trap, do you hear me?'

There were three of us and one of him. And we all knew instantly how stupid it would be to get involved in a fight with him. He was drunk and angry. I tried to calm him down.

'We're not filming your house, mate. We're just doing a couple of shots of Fiona.'

'Who the fuck asked you?' He lurched towards me. 'I'll fucking have you for filming my house.'

Fiona intervened. 'Jesus, will you leave it be? It's none of your fucking business. They're my friends. Leave it. Just stick to your business and I'll stick to mine.'

He stopped for a minute and stared at Fiona. He smiled. 'Listen to the fucking smackhead, eh! A fucking dirty smackhead is all you are.'

Fiona screamed back. 'They're my friends and you keep your fucking alkie nose out of it.' She was shaking and close to tears.

He turned to face me again. 'Has she told you all about how Kevin beats the shite out of her, has she? You can't blame him, mind you. Knocks the fuck out of her. No, she hasn't told you that lot, has she?'

'Just fuck off and leave us alone,' Fiona shouted back.

I told her we'd go away and meet her later. The drunk moved as if to go back to his flat. But before leaving he turned to shout a final insult. Fiona was fiddling with the lock on her front door. 'Smackhead. Smackhead,' he roared. Fiona ignored him. It was the voice of the playground bully and in a few seconds he was gone, vanishing behind the door of his flat.

Afterwards I asked her about her neighbour. He was just a drunk, she said. I wanted to ask her about Kevin, if what had been said was true. But she was shaken and humiliated, and I let the matter drop.

Fiona needed to score at least twice a day. Morning and afternoon. Her life was focused entirely on getting the money and the gear. Nothing came before that. Trying to track her down was an exercise in frustration. I would leave messages at the flat or with other addicts. I would torment Jacob with messages for her. Then one afternoon I was sitting in my study in London when the phone rang.

'Hi, Fergal, it's Fiona.'

'How are you? Where are you?'

'I've been in hospital. I had a blood clot in me leg.'

'How did it happen?'

'It came from me injecting in my groin. The clot travelled around and ended up in the leg. The doctors said if it happened again I could die.'

For all this grim news, she sounded happy. 'You know something, Fergal?' she asked.

'What is it?' I replied.

'I'm clean. I've been clean for seven days.' And there was more. 'I've split up with Kevin. He weren't treating me right, so I've left him. I'm staying at me mam's. I really want to get clean for good this time.'

I made an appointment to meet her in Leeds the following Monday morning. Part of me believed she would never appear. There were five days to go. In the life of a recovering addict five minutes can be an eternity, let alone five days. She would have picked up and started using again by the time I got to Leeds. Or she would have gone back to Kevin. One way or the other I never expected her to show.

It was bitterly cold, and I sat in the car with the heating turned up and the radio playing. *Why does it always rain on me? Is it because I lied when I was seventeen?* The song was by Travis, a Scottish band, and I will always think of it as Fiona's song. A song for the sad estates and for all the people who vanish into them. *Why does it always rain on me?* It was still playing when I noticed a small hunched figure walking up the hill past the red brick fortress of the old Mabgate Mills. It was Fiona, wrapped up in an oversized rainjacket and puffing away on a cigarette. From where I sat she looked so determined, so full of purpose, that nobody would have imagined she was a junkie pulled back from death's door only a few days earlier.

Up close she looked pale and tense. The hospital had been really tough with her, she told me. If she didn't stop using, she was dead. As simple as that. 'I really want to. I want to do it for me mam. I've put her through so much pain, I have to call a halt to it.'

She had a court appearance later that morning. She said Kevin was coming to pick her up. He would give her a lift to court. Somehow or other he was back on the scene.

A few days before I'd heard that an old woman who'd been mugged in the lift of one of the towers had become so afraid that now she wouldn't leave her son's house to go back to her flat. It was the second time Lucy Collinson had been mugged in a period of a few months. All her friends at the day-care centre believed it was a young junkie who'd carried out the attack.

'Why are addicts attacking defenceless old women, Fiona?' I asked.

'I would never do that. Never,' she replied.

'But it was somebody like you, an addict, who did it.'

'Well, I just know I'd never do that.'

'But why would somebody do that to an old lady?'

'You don't know what it's like. When they want the drug that bad, they'll do anything to get it.'

Fiona had stolen from shops and she had sold her own body. Addicts like her were mugging and robbing across Leeds. But I couldn't help liking her. She had a child-like sense of humour and was endlessly self-deprecating. And that morning in Lincoln Green I really did believe she was serious about going straight. She explained that she and

Kevin had gone through a bad patch and they'd moved out of the flat. The cops had raided it in the meantime. For now, she planned to stay with her mother. She and Kevin were just friends these days. After about an hour Kevin came driving up and sat waiting in the car with the engine running. He nodded towards me, the eternal cigarette dangling from his mouth. And then they drove off to court, where the case was adjourned.

About two months later I was walking down the high road near my home in London when my mobile phone rang, the screen flashing up a number in Leeds. It was Fiona.

'I just said I'd give you a ring to let you know how I'm doing.'

The truth was that she wasn't doing too well. Not very long after I'd last seen her, Kevin had been admitted to hospital. He had a perforated ulcer and was seriously ill. But even in that perilous state his craving for a fix was so overpowering that he left the hospital in search of a score. He found what he was looking for and died from an overdose.

'And how are you doing?' I asked Fiona.

'I'm back on it. I went back after Kevin died.'

I didn't bother to remind her of what the hospital had said. Dead like Kevin if she kept it up. One blood clot already, how many more chances would she get? I didn't say it, because Fiona didn't need me to tell her the score. She was one of the few addicts I'd met who didn't surround themselves with a blanket of denial. Fiona knew the story, but the pain of giving up the gear was more than she could bear.

And so I told her to call the hospital and see if they could help. I told her to try to get herself into rehab. She said she was trying and would stay in touch. Then she gave me an address in Leeds, a new flat far away from Lincoln Green, and said I should call if I was in town. Months later I did call. The flat was in a low-rise development about six miles from the city centre. I recognized it because it was the only one in the block with the curtains still drawn at midday. Through the letterbox I could see a single letter from the DSS addressed to Miss Fiona Stewart. But though I knocked and knocked, there was no answer. And she hasn't telephoned since. Nor has Jacob heard from her. As far as he knows, she is out there somewhere. Jacob is sure he'd have heard if anything had happened to her.

Going back over my notes of our first meeting, I saw that I had copied down two pieces of writing on the wall of her living room. The first was the Valentine's Day poem Kevin had written for her when he last came out of jail.

> Oh my Sweet Valentine, Fiona you are mine.
> I've been away all alone, on the 14th I've come home.
> On this special day to my Lord I did pray.
> Just being home with you again has eased the hurt and pain.
> These words are from the heart, how I hope we'll never
> part.

Behind the poem was a child's drawing. It was a series of concentric circles. I think it represented the sun and the moon together. The message read simply: 'To Daddy.' It was from Kevin's seven-year-old son.

## 5. Seeing the Waves

*They go to the seaside, Kath Barber and her gang of kids. She is the youth leader on Lincoln Green and the kids love her. I mean 'love' in the sense that these tough kids smile when she walks into the room. They trust her. She has this building behind the shopping centre where the kids come after school and weekends. The council gives her some money but nowhere near enough; the rest of what's needed she gets, or tries to get, from private donations. When the kids go on trips to the sea or the countryside she holds collections. On the wall of the Youth Base is a big notice with the names of donors, the amounts they've given towards the next trip. She is thin and sinewy, with dark black hair, piercing green eyes and a country woman's laugh. A handsome woman living on her own with her kids, Kath comes from rural North Yorkshire but has made the welfare of the children of Lincoln Green her life's work.*

*Kath and a group of children travel to this beach on the north-east coast and everyone jumps out of the bus and starts chasing around and shouting. The wind is blasting in from the North Sea, and the waves are crashing up on to the foreshore. The waves are brown and murky, thick with sand they've gathered on the long roll to the shore. Beach fishermen love these waves for the worms and crabs they churn up from the seabed, food to draw fish into the shoreline. But what does it look like if you are a kid who hasn't seen the sea before? As Kath is walking towards the shore, one boy grabs hold of her leg and won't let go. He is shaking with fear. He's a boy of about seven. She is having to walk with the kid hanging on to her leg. Then Kath notices a puddle of water forming at the kid's feet. And it hits her that he's pissing himself. It was only later she found out that he'd never been to the beach before, that he'd never seen the sea or waves. And she's still meeting kids like that. The north-east coast might as well be the Congo.*

The train had stopped at Grantham on the way back from Leeds when Kath Barber's story dislodged a memory from my childhood. I was seven years of age when the parish priest decided to take us on a trip to the seaside. The 'us' in question was a gang of kids who belonged to a youth club in the parish where I lived in Dublin. We were a mix of middle- and working-class kids. By that stage my family had moved out of the council estate in Finglas on the far northern fringes of the city into our own red-brick in the middle-class suburbs. We had escaped. The working-class kids in the club came from the older council estates that had been built soon after the foundation of the Irish Free State. These kids went to different schools from mine. I was wary of them.

Sometimes on the way to school a lad called Deco – I can't remember his surname – would spring out and demand money from me. He was a lot smaller than me but quick with the boot and fist. When Deco encountered someone like me he must have seen easy meat: a college boy in dark purple blazer and cap, bus fare rattling in my pocket and fear beaming out of my eyes. A weed. I didn't need to be warned to stay away from Deco and his mates. I almost never went to the youth club. I was shy and awkward, and had no intention of making it easier for them to single me out. And when I changed my route home, cutting down the lane way behind the Georgian houses on Eaton Square, I was able to avoid them altogether. Until the trip to the seaside. I think my mother felt it would be a good idea if I mixed more with other kids in the neighbourhood. I doubt that I signed up willingly for the trip.

When I got to St Joseph's Church, one of the first people I saw, waiting among a gang of about thirty boys, was Deco. But he paid no attention to me. If anything, he seemed nervous, unsure of himself. Surrounded by this large group of jostling and shouting boys, he was a much smaller figure.

We were loaded on to a bus headed for the Wexford coast. I have no memory of the journey, which I take as confirmation that nothing bad happened. I survived the initial contact without being spotted as a potential victim. It was night by the time we reached Wexford. We ran off the bus, shouting like lunatics. I remember the night air was warm and the smell of cut hay drifted from the fields behind the caravan park. The sea was about fifty yards beyond the last line of caravans, and that night – a gang of us crammed into a small van – we fell asleep to the sound of waves breaking on the beach below. I am left with the vaguest of fragments. Corned beef sandwiches and tea boiled on an open fire, sing-songs at night:

> Me ma was a lavatory cleaner,
> She cleaned them by day and by night,
> And when she came home in the evening
> She was covered in six feet of . . .
> Shine up your buttons with Brasso,
> Shine up your buttons with Vim,
> Shine up your buttons with Brasso,
> It's only three ha'pence a tin.

There were endless games of soccer and long walks across the white sand and up into the dunes, where we pretended to be French legionnaires fighting the Arabs. The first morning we all ran down to the beach and went screaming into the water. The youth workers were legging after us and warning us to go easy. I was jumping around and splashing with the rest of them, when I heard a voice calling out: 'Come on, Deco, it's fuckin' brill.' It was one of Deco's mates. Back on the shore, Deco was standing on his own, staring at the water. He was afraid to come in! I registered the sight and launched into an extravagant display of breast and back strokes and crawls. Deco stayed at the water's edge that day, and for the next two days he didn't come down to the beach at all, but stayed in the caravan playing cards with the other non-swimmers.

On the last day I was walking down to the beach with one of the youth club leaders, and I asked him why Deco wasn't swimming. 'I don't know. Maybe it's his first time at the seaside. I don't know.' I thought that unlikely. I had been to the seaside lots of times. There were plenty of beaches around Dublin. Sandymount. Dollymount. Port-marnock. Why couldn't Deco's ma or da have taken him swimming? I knew nothing about his life, but with the logic of a seven-year-old decided that Deco was a coward at heart. Mind you, that didn't embolden me to confront him and seek revenge for past attacks. But I did resume my old route home from school, and Deco never again came near me.

The possibility that Deco hadn't been to the seaside never figured in my calculations. Everybody went. As soon as the June holidays came, we were always being taken off to swim in the cold waters of Dublin Bay. On really hot days you would see crowds of kids from the inner city diving from the locks into the Grand Canal. I thought they did it because they were hard men; the idea that going to the beach wasn't a practical possibility for them, I never considered.

It wasn't until years later, when I was doing a part-time

job on a bread round, that the reality of being stuck in the city for a long, hot summer came home to me. I wasn't locked in myself; come August and I'd be off to the coast. It was the kids on the estates I travelled through every day who were trapped. The owner of the bread round, Ger Thunder, was an old friend from Finglas days. His mother was Breda Thunder, who'd looked after my brother and me when we were toddlers. The Thunders had escaped from Finglas too, moving into one of the bright new estates of semi-d's that were sprouting up along the city's western fringes.

Ger had followed his da into the bread business, a rough grind that involved unearthly (for me) starts at half past five in the morning. I never imagined it possible to hate the smell of fresh baked bread, but it happened. Day after day, groaning under the weight of the bread trays, I staggered from the bakery dispatch area out to Ger's van. The other drivers regarded me as a middle-class dosser, but Ger was patient and funny. His patience was an important asset on the summer roads of north Dublin. There were armies of bored kids who would chase the bread van, some of the tougher ones throwing stones at us, all of them with an eye to stealing a sliced pan or a batch loaf. They weren't robbing from hunger, just boredom. Ger would shout an endless variety of threats and insults at them: 'I'll fuckin' splatter ye if ye come near this van, ye little bollix' or 'You on the corner, ye have a face like a boiled shite, now fuck off home to yer ma'. I would stand behind him and do my best to look tough. He never hit anyone. The threats were always enough. The estates we drove around were places where Ger's father, Liam, had blazed a trail years before. The old man was known and respected. And Ger had the street cred to give a warning and be believed. Had I tried any of those lines, I'd have been taken asunder.

I hadn't thought about this stuff for years. The memories of Ger Thunder's bread round, the humiliation of Deco, all of it thrown up by the story of Kath Barber's trip to the beach. Actually, not only the story she'd told but everything Kath and her army of kids were fighting for among the tall towers of Lincoln Green. I doubt if the hard men of my childhood would have looked all that hard if you'd set them down in Lincoln Green. Not that the circumstances for 'alienation' weren't there on our estates: rising unemployment, families crammed into tower blocks with no facilities. But we lived in the age before heroin washed through the housing estates of Dublin. Drink was our curse, but it was legal; it didn't create big criminal gangs and it didn't pull young kids into early addiction the way heroin would a decade later.

The kids on Lincoln Green were living in a world where taking hard drugs from the age of thirteen (in fact, often younger) was part of growing up. And if they weren't taking the stuff, they could still see the detritus of heroin use scattered on the ground outside their homes. Old needles, discarded foil wrappers, junkie vomit.

Kath Barber arrived in Lincoln Green after a career that included working for Welfare Rights, Marks & Spencer and the RSPCA. She'd had lots of jobs. None of them was up to much but she'd do anything rather than go on benefit. When I asked what motivated her to take on the tearaways of Lincoln Green, she laughed. 'Oh, I don't know. Maybe naivety, idealism and all that.' And the experience of being a young mother on a big estate where there were no facilities for kids. Kath could see for herself what unemployment, drug addiction, alcoholism and family breakdown were doing to the kids on her estate. And so she started working there before moving on to Lincoln Green in 1991.

When she arrived, the estate was, in her own words, being held to ransom by a gang of young kids. They were hanging around on street corners, abusing passers-by, bullying the younger kids, extorting money. The council wanted something done, and so they hired Kath Barber. 'They were out of control. The community wanted rid of them. Everybody blamed the kids. It was all their fault. But the truth is that they were used as scapegoats for all the other problems going on. And, let's face it, this place isn't exactly child-friendly, is it?'

There had been an attempt at running a youth club but it was based in a school. By the time they'd finished a day's schooling, few of the kids were enthusiastic about going back in. At the start Kath worked from a flat on the estate. There were no ready-made premises to move into; most of her time was spent out on the streets just talking to the kids, getting to know them and where they were coming from. She always made a point of asking them what *they* thought a youth club should be about. At first the kids didn't want to know. Kath was just another adult coming snooping into their lives. But she kept talking and listening. After a while she was allowed to recruit a couple of part-time workers who helped her to organize trips to the park and the swimming baths. All of a sudden the kids of Lincoln Green had places to go. The council came up with premises: four old garages in a narrow square behind the shopping centre. But a lot of the locals told her she was wasting her time. It was money down the drain. It wouldn't last five minutes. Those kids won't appreciate it. When you meet Kath Barber, when you follow her around as she encourages, jokes, scolds and listens to the kids, you realize what an absolute waste of time it would be to try to persuade the woman out of anything.

She started out with just a few kids, but it grew and grew until she had thirty coming to the Youth Base on a regular basis. Word spread that Kath Barber was decent: if you told her something she didn't blab it to the world. The Youth Base was a safe place. Whatever time of the day you called in, Kath would be there to listen to you. And if you were a kid growing up in a drunk or drugged household, or in a place where the adults communicated through shouts and blows, the Youth Base was the one refuge you could depend on. Homeless kids often pitch up. The workers listen to their stories and attempt to persuade them to trust the authorities. The kids paint and draw, they play ball games and learn how to use cameras, they work on computers and have even made their own short video. The building is long and narrow, but the pokiness is compensated for by the bright murals the kids have painted on the walls. In the nine years she's been operating, Kath Barber hasn't recorded a single incident of vandalism. At the time I visited the Youth Base, the *Newsnight* programme on BBC 2 was reporting the chronic vandalism on a council estate in Salford outside Manchester. I was struck deeply by the image of a teacher weeping as she explained how the vandals had broken into the computer room and wreaked havoc. It wasn't just Salford. There were plenty of estates around the country where you could hear stories of wanton destruction.

The question of 'What on earth to do?' about the generation of uneducated and unemployable youth on the sink estates had reverberated through the political debate of the country for a long time. At various times and depending on the political climate, we wanted them locked up in boot camps, investigated by task forces, given jobs and good schools, taught respect for old-fashioned values. Kath Barber had listened to all the debates and emerged with what you might describe as a patient, liberal pragmatism. She believed in starting small, in her case a flat on the estate. The key was to keep coming back, no matter how much the kids tried to reject or evade you. And in time you gained their trust. The trick was not to pity them or be intimidated by them. And when you threw someone out for bullying, they stayed out. It had only happened once in the history of the Youth Base. You were the person they looked up to, but you were not the Big Boss. If there was trouble − say a kid was throwing his weight around, or somebody stole something from someone else - then a council was called. People had their say and things were sorted out by majority agreement. The kids themselves established the ground rules for the Base, said Kath. 'No swearing, no bullying, no racism. The stuff that is fundamental to make people feel comfortable.' And it could take weeks and weeks of repetition until the kids got the message.

I was there once when a kid had been bullied. The incident had happened around the corner, but the bad feeling had spilled into the Base. I was in the office with Kath when I heard a man's voice calling out. 'Oy, you two. Stop it now.' It was Kath's co-worker Mick. Kath jumped up and went outside. I heard her addressing one of the kids: 'Now look, Matthew. Just think, will ya? Just think about what you're doin'?' Kath and Mick took the victim and perpetrator to one side. They talked and talked. Nobody shouted, but the tone of Kath's voice was deadly serious. The bully had attacked another kid from behind. He was banned for the session. If you were a bully, you had to make a choice: continue in your old ways and lose something you really enjoyed, or change your ways. To minimize the opportunities for messing, Kath and Mick made sure the kids were kept occupied from the moment they arrived after school until the time they left several hours later.

Kath didn't think there was anything complicated about the success story of the Youth Base. 'Everybody is amazed, no vandalism, no destruction. But it's not hard to achieve it. The kids feel this place belongs to them. They know they're in control of their lives here. They know they get value from this. It's all about giving them a sense of ownership.' If I'd been hearing that word from a college lecturer or a psychologist, I'd be tempted to nod politely and yawn inwardly. And I've always been wary of so-called 'good news' stories, the 'bright shining beacon in the midst of despair' type of thing. But when a woman who has given up nearly ten years of her life to a place like Lincoln Green says 'ownership is the key', then I feel minded to pay her serious attention. Kath Barber knows what she is talking about. Once a session is underway, Kath and her workers break the kids down into small groups. That is another critical difference from school. The level of one-to-one contact is higher than a hard-pressed teacher with maybe thirty to forty kids would ever be able to manage.

The children who make it to the Youth Base are the lucky ones. They are just thirty-three kids out of a much bigger youth population on the estate. There were plenty of others out there. Some were in the nowhere land of drugs, others weren't allowed out after school for fear they'd meet drug dealers, others lived in homes where they acted as carers, where there wasn't the time to devote to the simple business of being a child.

One afternoon I saw a woman and a small child emerge

from one of the flats on the estate. The child was a toddler and it tottered around after the woman. She was arguing with a man who lived a few doors up. I didn't get the drift of what was going on, but I think he was complaining about noise. I described their appearance and asked Kath if she knew them, if there were kids from the family who came to the Youth Base. She didn't know them at all. A few days later I was on my way to see Kath when I met the woman and her child. She was walking around from the shops with two men, whom I took to be relatives. I asked if I could talk to them about life on the estate. 'No problem,' said the younger of the two men. He had lank blond hair, a thin face and spoke with a Glaswegian accent. He was carrying a can of Special Brew and walked ahead of the rest of the group. I noticed that the toddler was left to straggle behind, up the stairs and along the landing, until we reached the flat. Nobody looked behind to see if the kid was in fact following us. They just assumed he was there. At the flat a large black dog jumped out of the door to greet the Special Brew Man. 'Get the fuck down, will ye,' he shouted, smacking the dog across its muzzle. A girl of about five was waiting inside the flat. Long blonde hair, navy blue school uniform, a look of wariness as I followed Special Brew into the sitting room. There was a double bed in the room and people sprawled across it as they wandered in.

'What are you doin', then?' asked Special Brew.

I explained that I was trying to find out what it was like to live on Lincoln Green.

'It's fuckin' shite. That's what it is.'

He followed up his general statement of disgust with a detailed list of complaints. The council hadn't done this, that and the other. As the tirade gathered force, the little girl began to play with the dog.

The woman whom I'd seen arguing a few days earlier caught the dog by the scruff of the neck and hauled it away.

'But I want to play with 'im,' said the child.

'Away back to your mother's house and give us a bit of peace,' the woman said.

The girl came closer to the bed and began playing with the toddler.

'Are ye goin' to pay us?' asked Special Brew.

I said I didn't pay for interviews.

'That's a pity,' he said.

At this stage another woman arrived, carrying a newborn baby. She too sat on the bed. There were introductions, and then the young woman asked if I could get her on to *Who Wants to be a Millionaire?* I said no, and she seemed genuinely disappointed. The woman with the newborn baby was a friend of Special Brew's wife. Living in the house next door was Special Brew's sister. The little girl was her daughter.

I asked Special Brew how he'd ended up here in Lincoln Green. He explained that he'd come down from Glasgow to Leeds. He had been in trouble with the law up north.

What kind of trouble, I asked.

'Attempted murder,' he replied.

'Ah, right,' I said, as nonchalantly as I could manage.

'They couldn't make it stick on me for what I done, though,' he said.

*For what I done.* He sounded boastful as he recalled his victory over the forces of Scottish law. In the circumstances, I didn't pursue what sounded like an admission of guilt. I was, after all, here to listen to his account of life on Lincoln Green.

I asked him about the Youth Base. Did the little girl ever go there? He didn't seem to know anything about it. The Base wasn't far away, but, given his general state of awareness, I was inclined to believe that he truly didn't know of its existence. It is also possible that he might have regarded it as a haven of do-gooders, people who might cause him trouble.

'Do you mind if I go next door and talk to your sister?' I asked.

'Aye, no bother.'

Special Brew's partner wasn't so sure. 'She's not in a great mood, you know.'

I said I'd give it a try. The little girl followed us into the flat next door.

I explained myself all over again to her mother, a stocky woman with long brown hair. She barely glanced at me. She was sitting by the electric fire watching television. It was a game show, but I had the impression she had no interest in either the programme or my questions. Her answers were monosyllabic.

'What's it like living here with a small kid?'

'OK.'

'Is it hard to find things for her to do?'

'I dunno really.' After a few minutes I gave up and said goodbye. The little girl had gone back next door. As I was leaving the flats complex, a man came up and asked what I was doing. Another explanation. After hearing what I had to say, he told me the woman I'd just met was a hard case. The whole lot of them were always fighting with each other. And when they weren't fighting with each other, they were abusing the neighbours. He'd lived around Lincoln Green for nearly thirty years after coming over from Ireland. It hadn't started out as a rough place, but these days it was full of every kind of troublemaker. 'That lot next door are a holy fuckin' terror,' he said.

That was one side of Lincoln Green. Was it the predominant side? I honestly don't know. There was a lot to be depressed about on the estate. It was more than the unemployment figures and benefit statistics, a greater crisis than the terrible architecture or the needles scattered on the ground. The place stank of failure. It hung around the people like the smell of piss in the lifts. Kath Barber had smelled it and decided to push on regardless, one small project in the middle of all that social mess. But every time a new kid came through the front door of the Youth Base, Kath Barber claimed something back from the accumulated mass of failure. She'd used the Youth Base to fight for the rights of the kids and for the idea of community. Her way was public; it depended on the help of volunteers and what money she could bully out of the council.

But the fight was going on in other quieter corners of the estate too, behind the closed doors of flats and maisonettes, in the everyday routines of families who refused to accept the designation of failure that their address seemed to confer. It was there in the life 'Louise' described to me, a story that took months to reveal itself and that was hard to associate with the highly motivated young mother I met in the autumn of 1999. I met Louise and her children through the simple expedient of knocking on their front door. I'd spent the morning knocking on doors, mostly listening to complaints about the crime and the drug addicts. By the time I reached Louise, my head was spinning. Like everybody else she had to fidget with locks to get the door open.

But Louise was the first person to smile on seeing my face. 'Oh, I've seen ye going about taking notes. Come in.

Do you want a cuppa?' The flat was warm and well kept. I followed Louise into the sitting room, where a girl of about six was watching cartoons. Her other child, a boy aged ten, was at school and would be home in an hour, she explained.

Louise had lived in Lincoln Green for around five years. Before that she'd been in a flat in Chapeltown. At least in Lincoln Green her flat was on the ground floor, and it was near the shops and the launderette. There was even a tiny patch of garden out front. Her kids didn't have far to go to the Youth Base, and the bus stop was only five minutes' walk. 'Louise' is not her real name and I cannot give a physical description of her. She is still afraid of a family member who would hate her for telling the story of the childhood that brought her to Lincoln Green. Her life had been a series of sudden disruptions and escapes, pulled along in the wake of her mother and whatever man she happened to be living with.

Louise was born outside Hull and spent the first three years of her life in a small council estate. There were four of them: Louise, her sister and her parents. Her father left home before her third birthday, but she saw him twice a year until the age of seven. After that he disappeared from her life completely.

One night in the middle of her seventh year, Louise woke up to find the house on fire. Her mother had fallen asleep with a cigarette in her hand. 'I woke up in the middle of the night and there were this great big silly dog lickin' me face. And then this man comes in and lifts us all up and takes us to Pudsey with him. He was me mam's new boyfriend.' Until that night Louise had known nothing of the new man in her mother's life. He turned out to be a remorseless bully and child abuser. This is a story best told unmediated, in the words of the person who survived. All of this was described to me without a single tear, but in a voice that rushed to unburden.

*He were six feet three with thick black hair and a moustache. I don't know what he did for a livin'. I think he worked in a bakery for a while, but I can't remember any other jobs. He were the worst man I ever met. He used to beat us really bad. When me sister were about eight he raped her. But then she were dead clever. She went and done a lot of stuff wrong to get herself put into care. And when she were gone he started into me. I didn't know he'd started at her and she didn't know he'd been at me, not until recently when we started to talk about it. Me mam stuck with him for years, even though he used to beat her really badly and break her arm and nose. He had this big thick belt and he used to lash me and me sister with it. He'd say, 'Who wants to go first, then?' I'd go to school and get changed for PE and all these kids would be sayin', 'Ooh, Louise, what 'appened to your back?' But nobody ever did nought about it. This was the eighties and nobody did nought. I never spoke directly to him, I never called him dad, though he wanted us to.*

*Some nights we used to listen to him raping her in middle of night. And if we tried to do anything about it, he used to beat us. So we'd just sit in our room and try not to listen, but it's hard when your mam is screaming. Until he started on me I didn't realize what were goin' on. When you're a kid you don't, do you? His excuse were that I had to do what me mam wouldn't do. He said never to tell her because she wouldn't believe me. It were usually when me mam were off doing stuff with other blokes. Me real dad, like I say I used to see him on and off till I were about seven. I remember going to see him and he'd take me to a place in Hebden Bridge where there's a big forest and stepping stones and stuff. He used to take me to a café where we'd have macaroni* cheese. *I used to go for walks with him. Me dad's mental state of mind were bad and social services wouldn't let him mind us.*

At this point Louise's young son arrived home from school. She told him to go ahead into the sitting room and play a computer game. Tea would be ready in about an hour. He was blond and blue-eyed like his mother. Louise continued with her story.

*He don't know nothin' about any of this. The first time I went into care was when me mam beat me really bad. He said I'd stolen the key to his wardrobe but I 'adn't. Me mam said, 'If you tell us the truth we won't hit ye.' I was so scared I pretended I knew where it was. But as I was looking for it the two of them was beatin' me all the time. I were eight and a half. Someone told social services. After a while they said, 'Do you want to go back home?' And I thought that if I went home he wouldn't bother me mam as much 'cos he'd be bothering me. I just wanted to protect her. A social worker said to me mam, did she know her daughters had been sexually abused? She swore blind nothing had happened.*

*Me sister was already in care. That happened 'cos one night she takes me out with her and she robs a horse. She'd always had this thing about having a horse, hanging around stables a lot. So she goes to a field and takes one. We were walking up the road with this horse and these people come runnin' saying 'Get off me horse.' She ran off and left me, and the cops came and brought me home. Janie went into care for good after that. I really missed her.*

*When I were about ten, me mam left him for another guy in Pudsey. Why did she stick with him for so long? I could never understand that. The new one were a really nice guy. It were a nice house and me mam used to clean it for him and cook meals. But me mam drank all the time, every day. He were good to us at first. I think it was she changed him. He started drinking. This guy had a friend who were a lodger and he thought he could do what he wanted with me. I hated him, he were awful, sleazy and horrible. I were about thirteen year old. He used to give me money to keep me quiet. I don't know why I took it. I feel like I was a prostitute or something. He preyed on me 'cos he knew mam never gave me nothin'. He used to give me lifts to school and be really nice to me. I really knew what I were doin' was wrong. I saved up the money, and one day I went into town and bought a pair of shoes. I really needed new shoes. But me mam thought I'd stolen them and she really beat me up bad. I knew she wouldn't believe me if I'd told her the truth. Later on I stole stuff once or twice but not then. After that beating I were taken back into care.*

*I was scared when I went into care but I got to love it. It were a big old house in the city the first time, and then this kind of country mansion. They looked after me, they didn't tell you off all the time or beat you. I stayed in care until I was eighteen, for five years in three different homes. There were a lot of kids and there was some fights, but I loved it. We had a personal key worker who dealt with you. Was I lonely? Oh no. It were like heaven. I were glad to be there; it was so weird to wake up and not be scared. For a long time I thought I'd imagined it all, like I had a really vivid imagination or something.*

*When I was in care me sister had a baby. She was livin' in a flat, but she wasn't really able to take care of it. So I ran away from care to help her. That's when I used to go robbing stuff. It were all for the baby, nappies and stuff. In the end Janie couldn't look after the baby and it were taken for adoption. I loved that baby. I used to mind it all the time for her. She's thirteen now, you know, but I don't know where she is.*

In Louise's sitting room there is a photograph of the girl. It was taken when she was five years old and sent on to a third party by the adoptive parents. She is a pretty child, with the blue eyes of her aunt and a wide, untroubled smile. It was while she was in care that Louise met her future partner. 'Jonno' was a handsome boy, popular with everybody. He could mitch off from classes, get caught smoking and still never get into trouble. Jonno made Louise laugh, he protected her and at the age of sixteen he got Louise pregnant. She wasn't his only pregnant girlfriend. And a few months later he was sent to prison for six months for burglary. When he came out the two of them settled into a council flat in Gipton. Some time the following year Jonno found out he had cancer and went on chemotherapy. Louise nursed him while she was pregnant with her second child. But they fought all the time. 'He were fuckin' loopy with all the drugs he were takin'. We were screaming at each other mornin', noon and night.' They moved from flat to flat across Leeds before ending up in this maisonette in Lincoln Green, where their second child, the girl, was born.

Things went well in the beginning. Louise liked being on the ground floor; Jonno knew lots of people in the area, back to his old status as the handsome joker. They moved into Lincoln Green in the middle of summer in 1994. The problem was that Jonno couldn't get regular work with his illness. 'Employers wouldn't keep him on, so I went out to work. I got a job cleaning the pub in the morning and working at the bingo in the evenings and in between times I'd be lookin' after the kids. So it slipped into this routine of him doin' nothin' and me doin' everythin'. I were knackered.' They started fighting again. Jonno took to drinking. 'The thing was that I hated drink around the house 'cos of what happened when I were a kid. I just didn't want anybody in the house drinkin'. That were unfair on him and so he took to goin' out with his mates. I expected him to be the perfect dad and the perfect boyfriend, and he couldn't be. We fought over silly things. He'd go to take the toolbox down and start doin' something when I'd be making the tea and we'd end up in a huge argument.'

Then came Christmas and Jonno got 'mad' drunk. On his way home from the pub he got into a big argument with a gang of drug dealers across the road. For days Louise was terrified the gang would attack the house. She watched the door, kept peeking out of the window. And a few days after Christmas she asked him to leave. 'I realized I couldn't make him the person I wanted, so I asked him to go. He still comes to see the kids every week, but it's over between us.' The kids want to be with their father. The boy keeps asking Louise when he can go and spend some time with his dad. But his dad isn't always available, which is Louise's loyal way of saying that Jonno has a habit of not keeping his promises to the children.

Louise is mother, father and friend to these beautiful children. I went to see her four or five times and always came away with a warm, hopeful feeling. The house is calm. There is routine. Meals appear at regular times. Clothes are washed and ironed. Nobody is drunk or hits anybody. To supplement her benefit of £135 a week Louise works several hours a week at the local school, keeping an eye on the kids in the playground. She gets £15 for this – she isn't allowed to earn any more under the social security regulations. Her furniture, the children's shoes, Christmas and birthday presents she buys from catalogues. She is as determined about repaying the money as she is about every other aspect of her domestic life.

Though she likes her maisonette, Louise's plan is to move from Lincoln Green eventually. She wants her kids to do A-levels and go to university. 'It's all the stuff that goes on around 'ere that worries me. I keep lookin' at them and wondering which one will be the drug addict, which one of 'em will it get. I don't want to hang around in a place like this waiting to find out, do you know? So I've applied for houses in other places and I'm waiting to see. I'll get them out of 'ere, don't you worry.' I didn't doubt that she would.

Her sister Janie had moved from one care home to another. She'd had another baby but it died at the age of three months. Cot death. Then she met and married a man who beat and abused her, as every other man she'd been with had done. One day after he'd raped her she went to the hospital, where they discovered internal damage so bad there was no choice but to remove her womb. She left him after that. These days Janie is living with a kinder man. He never raises his voice, much less his fist. They have a nice house and two dogs. She and Louise are close, but they have never confronted their mother, or any of the men who inflicted abuse on them in childhood. Louise is still afraid of her mother. 'You'd think butter wouldn't melt in her mouth, honestly, but you've no idea what she's capable of.' When her mother comes to visit she is polite, she brings presents to her grandchildren, she takes them out on treats. I was there once when she came; a hard-faced woman in late middle age who shuffled about the room without ever making eye contact. Louise was quiet and deferential in her presence.

'Do you think you'll ever be able to face her with the past?' I asked Louise. It was the afternoon of my last meeting with her. The kids were in the sitting room watching television. 'I have tried to talk to her. But she just denies everything. She says I were the troublesome one. She goes on about me robbin' stuff and all, making out like everything that happened was my fault. Some day I will face her with it all, I know I will. It's just not easy, you know. She's very good to me kids too, she takes them out and buys them shoes and the like. It'll take time.'

As I was starting to write this book, a message came from Louise via a colleague who'd been speaking with her by phone. Louise had started a course at the polytechnic. Every week she sat in a class with a group of women learning how to be assertive. 'I've started,' she said to my colleague.

# 6. The Hill People

They lived on the side of a mountain. In winter the snow could maroon them for days on end. Great drifts of it shrouded the road and fields and every living thing on the ground. As Gwylithin described it, it was more silent than any quiet you've ever known. You would hear nothing at all except the bleating of sheep trapped on the mountain. At times like that Gwylithin could imagine that all the trouble in their life had been locked out. It was just her and Arwen and the three girls and nothing could come up the road to harm them.

The girls – Alau (ten), Maly (seven) and Nest (three) – followed their father Arwen out into the drifts. He wasn't so fond of the snow. He would have to spend hours on the mountain digging the sheep out and carrying them down to the barn beside the house. When the thaw came, the melted snow would flood the river that ran behind the farmhouse, sending the water cascading down into Arwen's pasture. In winter, tiny lakes formed in the centre of the field, pushing the small herd of cattle towards the hedgerow.

They were tenant farmers, people of no property who lived in the valley of Cwmpenanner – the valley of the Calf's Head. The narrow road came to an end outside their front door. Beyond the farm was rocky mountain and miles beyond that the Irish Sea. The ground was hard and flinty, and the rain seemed to fall incessantly.

I had come to north Wales in winter, travelling by railway

past silent coastal towns and inland to Llandudno Junction. I collected a hire car and drove the last hour to Arwen and Gwylithin's farm. It lay in wild-looking country, near one of the country's finest tourist attractions, the Snowdonia National Park. This was weekend country for large numbers of English and Welsh townspeople; many had holiday homes here, and the mountains of Snowdonia attracted climbers from all over the world. In villages like Betws-y-coed the commercial life depended on tourist money. Where Arwen and Gwylithin lived, however, there was no tourist trade. Their nearest village was Cerrigydrudion, which sat on the main road between Llandudno and Holy-head. 'When you get to Cerrig turn right and head up the mountain,' Gwylithin had told me on the phone. The road climbed steeply for a mile or so before levelling out to reveal a vast tract of countryside, upon which grazing sheep were dotted as far as the eye could see. The scraggy fields were subdivided by low stone walls. Closer to the road there were a few cattle gathering against the snipe grass that grew in tufts behind the walls. I drove past a ruined cottage on my right; further ahead on my left, a transmitter for mobile phones. It started to rain. At the highest point of the moun-tain there was a crossroads. The road that turned sharply down to the left would take me to Arwen and Gwylithin's farm.

I parked the car and looked down the valley. The writer and wanderer George Borrow had stopped to admire the view near here in 1854. Borrow was a romantic with a burning enthusiasm for Celtic folklore and traditions. Unusually for an English gentleman of the period, he had learned the Welsh language, which he insisted on practising with every peasant he met along his route. Near Cerrigydru-dion he encountered two children standing alone outside a 'wretched hovel' by the roadside. The exchange that followed is an illuminating piece of social history.

'Have you any English?' said I, addressing the boy in Welsh.

'*Dim gair*,' said the boy. 'Not a word. There is no *Saesneg*★ near here.'

'Have you a father and mother?'

'We have.'

'Are they in the house?'

'They have gone to Capel Curig.'

'And they left you alone?'

'They did . . .'

'Do you help your father and mother?'

'We do; as far as we can.'

'You both look unwell.'

'We have lately had the ague.'

'Is there much of it about here?'

'Plenty.'

'Do you live well?'

'When we have bread we live well.'

When we have bread. Rural poverty of the kind described by Borrow was commonplace throughout the United Kingdom of that period; in areas where the land was especially poor – north Wales, the west of Ireland, the Scottish Highlands – there was a remorselessly thin line between poverty and starvation. The tenant farmers around Cerrigydrudion were mostly renting from English landlords; if they could not make enough to pay the rent, they faced the threat of eviction. They had a reputation for thrift and hard work, as the social historian Sabine Baring-Gould recorded in his

★ *Saesneg*: English. The Welsh word is similar to the Irish *Sasanach*.

*Book of North Wales,* published in 1903: 'The women milk the cows, make the butter, and look after the marketing of lesser products, and work in the fields in hay and even harvest time. The men do all the outdoor work, only hiring labour, which as elsewhere in Wales is scarce and dear, when absolutely compelled to. Farmhouse fare is of a notoriously spartan kind all over North Wales, and nowhere more so than here. Fresh meat is rarely tasted.'

It was beautiful land, but you understood within minutes of arriving that it took a rare kind of toughness to make a living from it. The figures suggested very few were making a living. The body that represented the tenant farmers across the country had asked their members to calculate their earnings. The national average worked out at £2,000 a year. Ever since coming back to live in Britain, I'd been reading stories about the crisis in farming. It was a grim tableau: the BSE crisis, collapsing EU milk prices, vast overdrafts. Fifty-four farmers had committed suicide in 1998. In the midst of all this, the government had decided to ban hunting, a move that many in the farming community interpreted as an unwarranted assault on their livelihood and traditions. By the time I set out for north Wales the farming community was in a state of war with the Labour government. It was an argument that polarized urban and rural Britain: the city dweller was largely disinclined to sympathize with the farmers, the farmers saw themselves as victims of urban selfishness and complacency. Some liberal commentators showed a decidedly illiberal streak when it came to discussing the farmers: if they couldn't make it work, they should be left to go the way of the coal-mining industry. The newspapers of the right cast the Labour government and its European partners as the greatest threat to rural Britain since Hitler's armies menaced the coast in 1940.

It was a debate fuelled both by traditional animosities on both sides as well as by economic crises. But for the purposes of my journey, I had only to look at the financial realities of their existence – the miserable incomes, the huge numbers receiving income support and family credit – to conclude that tenant farmers were definitely people of the British margins, no less than the families who lived in the concrete prairies of Govan or Leeds.

My experience of farm life had been limited. I was a city boy and prey to the prejudices of a peer group that regarded country people as bumpkins. The fact that most of us were only a generation removed from the land was forgotten. Both my parents' families had come from farming stock. My father's people had a small dairy farm on the north Kerry coast where I'd spent idyllic summers. They were kind, hard-working people and they treated me well. But when I went back to the city to be met by jeers of 'redneck' and 'hairyback', I forgot any loyalty I might have had to my country cousins. At school we tended to be circumspect about jeering the country boys. I once made the mistake of mimicking a big fellow named Larkin; he overheard and brought his ham-like fist crashing into my jaw. That was the end of my mimicry. The country boys were tougher than us and we resented them for it.

As we got older, the resentment was deepened by the certain conviction that every farmer in Ireland was living off the fat of the land. The heavily taxed (48 per cent, top rate) middle classes saw the farmers as a greedy, subsidy-glutted élite who whined incessantly but contributed little to the nation's welfare. It was a view not dissimilar to that held by large sections of the British public when the farming crisis spilled on to their front pages and television screens at the end of the twentieth century. Though my own views had moderated, I still carried a residual suspicion of complaining farmers.

I told Gwylithin about this and she laughed. 'Give yourself time, see how we live, and then make a judgement.' She had red hair and bright green eyes; a broad-shouldered, stout woman who worried incessantly about her weight. She laughed a great deal. Sentences frequently trailed off into giggles. I suspect that a lot of the time her laughter was the result of embarrassment. Her people had always kept their troubles to themselves; whatever may have been true of other farmers, neither she nor Arwen had come from a culture of disclosure or complaint. But things had reached a stage where Gwylithin could keep quiet no longer. I'd been sent to see them by the local Farmers' Association; they were in deep trouble, I was told, and were willing to talk.

The house in which they lived dated back to 1560. They knew this because a group of local historians had turned up one day to look around the farm. People had been farming on the mountain for at least four centuries, they said.

It was a cold house that had never known central heating. Gwylithin lit big wood fires in the sitting room, but the cold lay in perpetual ambush beyond the narrow radius of the fire. There were three small bedrooms, a living room and a kitchen. Part of the upstairs ceilings and walls were mottled with damp. Most of the time Gwylithin and her children congregated in the kitchen around an old range they'd bought from a neighbour. At school she'd won lots of prizes for her cooking, and the kitchen invariably smelled of baking. Whenever there was a party or an *eisteddfod* at the chapel down in the valley, Gwylithin would be called into action.

The farmhouse and land were rented from an English landlord. They never said much about the landlord; they were dependent on his goodwill and understandably reluctant to talk about the relationship publicly. They saw him rarely, only when he came up during the season to shoot grouse. On the first day I met her, Gwylithin had just finished doing the accounts. It was a weekly ritual, the taking down of the big ledger and the realization that yet again they had failed to make ends meet. The family owed £30,000 to the bank, all of it borrowed to pay for livestock and machinery. Now the livestock was virtually worthless. Across Wales farmers were dumping sheep in public places in symbolic protests; there was an oversupply of sheep and the large supermarkets were essentially able to pay what they liked. And so the ewe that Arwen sold at 56 pence a kilo ended up costing the consumer £12.60 a kilo. It was a mark-up of over 2,000 per cent. The supermarkets could argue all they liked about hygiene, marketing, transport and labour costs, but they would never convince the likes of Arwen Jones that he wasn't being made a fool of. It was the law of supply and demand all right, and the big chains held all the power.

Ten years ago when Arwen and Gwylithin had come to farm, prices were relatively stable. They knew they would have to work hard, but there was a fair chance of a living wage. Now Arwen earned less than £80 a week. This was his return for a winter working day that began at seven in the morning and ended at nine in the evening; in summer he didn't get back to the farmhouse until half past midnight. It was his life seven days a week, fifty-two weeks a year. The couple were now receiving family credit of £104 a week. Arwen was ashamed of that, said Gwylithin. It made him feel like a failure. There were tens of thousands of tenant farmers in the same position across Britain, but that was scant consolation to Gwylithin as she waited for her husband night after night. 'He's like a robot. He's a work-aholic. It's not fair what life is doing to him. He just works, works, works, and you can't do that. He's OK now 'cos he's young, but give him ten, fifteen years I don't think he'll manage.'

Arwen wanted Gwylithin to get a job. But she wanted to be at home for the children. 'What would they do on their own up here in the school holidays? Who would meet them off the bus, at the end of the school day? It's not fair on them. They want to see their mum when they get home from school. It's hard to say this in the modern age, you know. But I feel I need to be here for them. I get their meals and do their homework with them. And I work here at home on the farm. If he is working on another farm or away at his other fields, I need to watch for the cow that is calving, and do all the other jobs around the farm.' Still, she'd signed up for a computer course just in case.

The children saw little of their father. 'They adore him, but they don't see him. I'm the one they try things on with, I have to discipline them. The good days are when he is home and I can help him outside. Sometimes you want an adult to talk to, but he's never around.' This was not said in an angry or bitter voice. Gwylithin was twenty-seven years old and lonely; by the time I met her in the last months of 1999, she was also starting to get very scared. If the bank decided that Arwen was wasting his time and the money wouldn't ever be repaid, they might decide to foreclose. And if that happened, the family owned nothing. The house belonged to someone else, the remaining livestock and machinery would be sold off by the bank. There was no collateral to allow them to start up again when the rural economy improved. And where would they go? To a council house in the village if they were lucky, with Arwen labouring on another man's farm, though with farmers going to the wall everywhere the work was by no means guaranteed.

Gwylithin divided her days into those she called 'good', 'bad' and 'very bad'. On the very bad days she cried all the time. The day before I called at the farm the doctor had prescribed anti-depressants. She tried to talk to Arwen about the problems on the farm, but he didn't want to face them. He just kept working hard, hoping things would change. 'He's proud,' she said. 'You know up here, you're not talking about nineties man. You're talking about 1890s man. They keep their troubles to themselves. I know it must be affecting him, but he doesn't want to face reality.'

I tried to talk to Arwen about the farm difficulties. He could give you the figures, but he avoided drawing any conclusions. He spoke in short sentences and then lapsed into long silences. Our conversations were painfully awkward. It was intimidating at first, and then you got used to his shyness and the deep worry that must have been filling every hour of his day. Instead I talked to him about rugby. He was a big man, six feet tall and broad, and he still occasionally played for the village team. He joked about how terrible the Irish team was and I agreed with him. One day he took me to the market and I saw that he was as quiet with his friends as he was with strangers. Mind you, there were very few talkative men at that market; there was an air of exhaustion – that is the only word that will do – about the whole place.

But at home with the children Arwen was transformed; he would gather them up in his arms when he walked through the door, smiling and asking questions about their day. He looked – how can I describe it? – almost carefree; and in those moments you could glimpse the young man who'd charmed Gwylithin on her seventeenth birthday at a barn dance for the Penyfed Sheepdog Association. 'Oh, the sparks flew, I can tell you. He had this lovely smile. I thought he must have been going with someone. But he asked me if I wanted a lift home and that was the beginning of it all.' They started going out, and Gwylithin became pregnant with Alau, their first daughter. The couple married in October 1993 and moved into a village house. But Arwen wanted to find a farm of his own. He was the son of an agricultural contractor who travelled around the farms with his JCB, digging ditches and repairing drains. Arwen had gone to agricultural college and then out to work as a farm labourer. He had been given two fields by his parents, and these he'd sold to get money for livestock. Now all he needed was a farm to rent.

One Friday evening Gwylithin's mother telephoned to say a farm had become vacant on the mountain. They phoned the land agent and he told them they could view Pentry-Mawr Farm the following Monday. Gwylithin knew the place well. Every curve of the mountain path on Pentry-Mawr was woven into her memory. Each summer of her childhood had been spent at the farm next door, where Gwylithin's grandmother lived with her son Ivor. She remembered summer lunchtimes and her grandmother's kitchen filled with hungry neighbours who'd come to help with the lambing; on Sunday mornings before chapel she would lie in her grandmother's bed, listening to fairy stories. Gwylithin's gran made her feel special. At home there were three other sisters competing for her mother's attention; on the farm she was her gran's pet. Eventually her uncle Ivor found a farm with better drainage further along the valley and they moved on; there were no more summer holidays at Pentry-Mawr.

She went back there with Arwen on a summer's day. There hadn't been rain for weeks and the mountain was dry, the grass brittle and shaded brown. The feeling as they walked around the land was 'something like magic', she said, like coming home at the end of a long, long journey. They moved in soon after. 'The day we were due to come, it was 14 October, and I was up at six in the morning, I was so excited. All the colours were turning on the hills. The furze was going from yellow to brown. Oh, it was magical.'

One afternoon I walked with Gwylithin to the top of the mountain. In a few days she and Arwen would come up to drive the ewes down to the sheds before taking them to market. She often came up here. The stony path took her away from her worries for an hour.

'Just stand quiet and listen,' she said.

I heard only the sound of the wind funnelling through the valley and, below that, faintly discernible, the noise of water rushing through the farm stream.

'You hear that? It's magic. I can stand here and believe I'm the only person in the world.'

Gwylithin began to name the farms dotted along the valley. They were the places where four generations of her family had reared their families. 'Over that way is uncle Hwyel, over there is uncle Wynne's place. That is where my grandmother grew up, and that was my uncle Ivor's farm.'

Gwylithin was reminding me how bound in she was to this land.

'What a place for children to grow up! They know the names of trees, birds and different breeds of animals. You don't get that in town. Up here you don't worry about what might happen to your kids the way people have to in the town. I love the life, that's the thing that conquers it.'

Weeks later I was reading an anthology of local writings when I came across a poem that Gerard Manley Hopkins had written while sitting at a waterfall not far from where Gwylithin and Arwen were farming. They were some of the most plaintive lines I'd read about the claims of land-scape on being.

> The sun on falling waters writes the text
> Which yet is in the eye or in the thought.
> It was a hard thing to undo this knot.

For Gwylithin and Arwen the knot was being pulled asunder before their eyes. Without money to pay the bills, the land and all it symbolized – childhood memory, the future of their children – was slipping away from them. It was hap-pening bit by bit, the incremental departure of dreams.

Back in the kitchen, I asked Gwylithin if she thought they'd survive.

'I want to stay here more than anything. But when the bills are coming in, you've got to be realistic. I don't see a future, not as it is.'

There were 320 acres. Arwen had followed the general advice of the time: you had to be big to have a reasonable chance of survival in modern agriculture. And for a while they seemed to be making a go of things – until the unholy trinity of BSE, falling prices and rising costs came creeping up the road and started to strangle the life out of the farm. Arwen rented more land – another 152 acres – to try to make the economies of scale work in his favour. But they didn't. He and Gwylithin were never a big spending couple, not in the sense of buying clothes and going out for meals or taking holidays. So when it came to economizing, there was very little fat to be trimmed from their lives. They went out exactly three times a year: on the night of Arwen's birthday, on the night of the Cerrigydrudion show, and on the Saturday before Christmas for a meal with the other farmers in the valley. As a rule they didn't go on holidays. The previous year they had taken two days off to take the girls to the seaside. They went to Caernarvon and walked around the castle. The girls wanted to go inside but the admission fee was more than their parents could afford. There was a choice of having their tea in a café or going inside the castle. The children didn't complain; according to Gwylithin, they rarely complain. They pick out clothes and toys in the catalogues Gwylithin keeps by the television, and hope that by some chance their father will bring home a windfall. 'I'd like to go to the cinema once or twice, but the cash isn't there for it,' she said. 'You think it would be easy to say we're going to set aside £10 for it every couple of weeks, but the money just isn't there for that. I'd much rather spend it on shoes for the children. Wouldn't you?'

I was in the house on the morning of Alau's birthday. Gwylithin had bought her a mirror and a bottle of sparkling nail varnish. The presents had cost £4.50 in the village store. Alau had wanted a compact disc by the pop group Steps, but she smiled and looked happy for her mother when she unwrapped the presents. Gwylithin said she and Arwen did their best to protect the girls from the stress they were both feeling. Alau smiled a lot, and mothered the two younger girls, but she hung around the edges of Gwylithin's conversations the way eldest children often do, and I was sure she knew exactly what was happening to the farm. And beyond the farm there were plenty of pointers to decline that an observant child could pick up.

Alau and her sister Maly went to the village school in Cerrigydrudion. Gwylithin's aunty Nan taught there. There had been four schools in the area until the 1980s. But there was no longer the farming population to support that number. Now there was one school.

Once, on a rainy day, I stopped at Ivor Jones's farm-supply store in Cerrig to buy wellingtons. The shop sold a bewildering mixture of clothes and fertilizers and small farming implements. An old lady behind the counter told me business was quiet. She spent a good fifteen minutes advising me on which wellingtons would be best suited to my feet; it was old-fashioned customer service, but I suspected too that she was glad of the company. Three months later, and again blasted by the wind and rain, I was back visiting Gwylithin and Arwen when I drove over to the shop, intending to buy a scarf. There was a notice in the window announcing that Ivor Jones was closing down. He was moving to Bangor for work. Ivor himself came out, a short young man with sandy hair. He said there just wasn't the business any more.

I left Ivor and walked up the road past the Lion Inn and the war memorial to the school. Aunty Nan was in her early fifties, a big warm woman who spoke in passionate, rolling phrases. She too was married to a struggling tenant farmer. There were eighty-six children in the school, boys and girls, and most of the boys she taught wanted to be farmers. As I walked in, I heard the sound of children singing. It was a Welsh hymn, 'Dim on Seren' ('The Last Star'), and the fingers on the piano were those of Nan Owen. I've always believed you could tell fairly quickly if a school was a happy place or not. Riotous, frantic schools are not happy. They are places where weaker children get singled out and bullied; nor are schools happy places if kids walk around with their heads bowed and try to melt into the wall to allow you to pass. Nan Owen's school was neither of these. There was a sense of order, but they were lively and, for the most part, smiling children. Most came from farming families, a fact that presented Nan with difficulties when it came to the issue of career guidance.

'A lot of these children want to be farmers, like their parents and their grandparents. And you don't just tell them no, you can't be a farmer. You tell them that farmers need to be educated these days, that they must go on and get qualifications, a farmer needs to be a scholar with all these forms to fill in and so on. And in that way you hope they will be ready.'

But was that telling them the truth about the future?

'Oh no. But what should I say? Should I tell them that there won't be a farming community at Cerrigydrudion? Don't even think about farming, children? I couldn't break their little hearts like that. No.'

Nan Owen could see the bigger picture. She watched what was happening to young couples like Arwen and Gwylithin and then tried to look ahead a decade or so. What she saw was the vanishing of a community: the hills and valleys where her people had given generations of their labour would no longer be able to sustain them.

'It saddens me. Along with the farming there is a culture. There is our Welsh language and our sense of community. That is dwindling now. You see, children in a school like this get a special identity. They get a sense that they belong. They say "yes", I'm part of something. And if there are no children here, there will be no school. No school' – and here she pauses – 'at Cerrigydrudion.'

I met Nan again the following Sunday at the Methodist

chapel. The tenant farmers of the valley had worshipped here for more than a hundred years. It was a small congregation, mostly the older people and Gwylithin and her three girls. Arwen and the majority of the men were out working on the mountain. The service was held in one of the side rooms normally used for Sunday School. There was a table on which the preacher had placed his Bible. In front of that were two small heaters. The preacher was a visitor, a genial young man with curly hair and thick glasses whose voice rose and fell in the style of an old-fashioned revivalist. He spoke for an hour, the preaching punctuated by hymns. Gwylithin's youngest daughter became bored and took out a small comb, stroking her mother's red hair. The service was in Welsh, and so I couldn't follow what was being said. I was told later that he had asked the people to have courage in their times of difficulty. Just beyond the preacher's head there was a window through which I could see sheep grazing on the mountainside. By the end of the service, the air in the room had thickened and covered the window in condensation, and it was no longer possible to see the valley or the animals.

# 7. Faithful Departed

Ron Roberts had a long story to tell. It was as old as the century and crowded with the voices of a vanished country. When you met Ron and listened to him, it was hard to recognize him as a citizen of the new Britain. He was the son of a Boer War veteran and had fought in the Second World War. In his speech and manners, but most of all in his gentleness, he was a rarity. Courtly and self-deprecating, a gentleman. Since Gracie died he's been living on his own. Once a week his two daughters came to visit, and his son-in-law who drove a taxi called in whenever he could.

His flat was on the second floor of a red-brick mansion block, next door to Pentonville Prison on the Caledonian Road. The neighbourhood was one of the poorer parts of London's borough of Islington. On the other side of the road, behind the mail office and the Methodist church, were several acres of the ugliest urban settlement in the capital: block after block of flats into which Islington's poor and who knows how many refugee families had been crammed. The refugees had come from everywhere – Somalia, Ethiopia, Kosovo, Bosnia – fleeing war and poverty in the last chaotic decade of the twentieth century.

Compared to the sad tower blocks, the mansion block where Ron Roberts lived was a model of architectural beauty. It was low rise with the flats built around a small courtyard. There was a playground for children in the courtyard and several trees that gave the place an air of calm quite at odds with the surrounding neighbourhood.

I drove around the back and parked next to an Ethiopian restaurant. A man standing outside said he'd keep an eye on the car. 'The kids here, man, you got to be careful with 'em.' The only kids I met were a group of boys who were kicking a football around in the archway that led into the flats. There were three of them, about ten years old, and they spoke in a foreign language I vaguely recognized. A Balkan language, I think.

I had an old friend from South Africa staying with me that weekend. Milton Nkosi was a Soweto-born journalist with whom I had covered the end of apartheid and the election of Nelson Mandela to power. 'Come and see the other London,' I'd said to him that morning, as we walked the high street near my home. 'It isn't all Starbucks and Waterstone's.' As it happened, Milton knew the area. He'd stayed in a flat here for several months in the mid nineties while attending a training course in the West End.

'So, baba, we're heading for the townships, your British townships,' he'd joked as we drove up past King's Cross in the direction of the Caledonian Road. It was a joke, but it pointed up an uncomfortable truth. Where I lived in a leafy suburb of west London, you were as insulated from the realities of marginal Britain as any white South African was from the trials of township life. The nearest council estate was two blocks away. But I had no reason to go there. I suspect I was no different from most of the middle-class residents of my west London suburb.

I knew that *they* were out there. Mostly it was a question of following trails left in the night. The glass glistening beside a car with a shattered window; the butt end of a spliff or an empty Special Brew can in the kids' playground. One morning I came outside to find the police surrounding a group of kids in a car. There were five youngsters, average

age about fourteen, and they'd been caught driving a stolen car. I looked inside and saw a tangle of torn wires, a screwdriver, a wrench, some cigarette ends and bits of cardboard ready to be made into a spliff. The kids were laughing among themselves. I don't think it was bravado. Whatever was happening genuinely did not worry them. They doubtless calculated that they would be arrested and charged, and back on the streets in a matter of hours. Nothing the police said or threatened them with seemed capable of puncturing their defiance.

Ron Roberts was afraid of kids like that. At eighty-three years of age and with badly failing eyesight, he rarely ventured out. There was no problem in the block where he lived, but outside the gate it was hard to know who might be waiting to attack you. Unemployment in Islington was nearly twice the London average, and there were estates in the borough that had earned a reputation for violent crime as notorious as any in the country. And if ever you wanted a clear example of the link between crime and poverty, you needed only to compare the crime figures for Islington with somewhere like Kensington and Chelsea in the west. In the first month of the new millennium there were 404 crimes of 'violence against the person' in Islington compared to just over half that number in Kensington. When I visited Ron Roberts, it was very easy to see why he would feel afraid to walk the streets on his own.

Yet Islington was not one vast urban waste land. Anything but. The borough contained some of the most desirable addresses in London, if you had the money. A three-bedroom house cost £500,000, the asking price for a two-bedroom flat was between £250,000 and £350,000. Even on the Marquess Estate, former council flats were now fetching up to £160,000. A local estate agent was quoted as saying that architects had taken to buying flats in tower blocks in Clerkenwell, attracted by the top-floor views. The high crime, the worst GCSE results in London and the high unemployment sat cheek by jowl with neighbourhoods of conspicuous wealth. The other Islington was a place of shiny restaurants and bars, with some of the highest house prices in the capital. It was also the heartland of New Labour, where Tony Blair and Gordon Brown were reputed to have agreed their political strategy in a restaurant called Granita, a shrine to chic minimalism on thriving Upper Street.

I was sitting in a coffee bar on Upper Street when I came across Ron Roberts's story. One of the local papers, the *Islington Gazette*, had reported that Ron had had to spend his life savings to pay for an eye operation. Delays in the NHS could have meant a wait of several months and Ron wasn't in a position to hang about.

Ron had lived in the block for twenty-two years. For all but the last three months he had shared the flat with his wife Gracie. She died at Christmas time. He had created his own small garden on the landing outside the flat. There was a green wooden gate and behind it a profusion of flowers and bedding plants. All in all, the landing space wasn't more than a few feet wide, but Ron had transformed the look of the place; when you walked through the gate it really was possible to imagine the flat was a cottage in the heart of the country. Since his wife had died, Ron hadn't bothered with the garden. He didn't have the energy or the inclination. What was the point? he asked himself.

Inside, the flat was conspicuously plush, a place that felt like it had been well looked after. The carpeting was thick, and the hand of his late wife could be seen in the velvet drapes of the sitting room and the floral designs of the couches and armchairs. It was comfortable in an old-fashioned way with numerous ornaments – China soldiers, a small crystal galleon – crowded on to the shelves. He built the bookcases and shelves himself. By trade he'd been a carpenter and until recently had done all the odd jobs around the house. In a place of honour at the centre of the mantelpiece was a portrait of Gracie. The woman in the photograph was in her fifties with a bouffant hairdo. She wore a long gown and was standing on a spiral staircase. Around the frame he had draped a gold necklace and a pair of earrings. The photograph had been taken on their wedding day more than twenty-two years before.

Ron was a distinguished-looking man, with a neat moustache and large brown eyes. For the past two months, in fact since soon after Gracie died, these eyes had been giving him trouble. When he went outside the light blinded him. He would try to cross the road and not see cars coming and the motorists would shout at him. So he would find someone crossing the road and walk behind them. He did the same thing walking down to the shop, always walking in someone's shadow so that he could be sure of not falling. When he tried to read the papers the letters and images blurred. He had two big magnifying glasses beside his chair in the sitting room. With these and his glasses he struggled to read the newspapers or the letters that arrived from the electricity people or the hospital. When you added to this his angina and his bad hearing, Ron had every reason to feel vulnerable when he walked down the Caledonian Road. He was afraid of the traffic, afraid of strangers, afraid of the gangs who might see an elderly man stumbling home with his pension as an easy target. 'Oh, drug gangs. There's lots of gangs around here,' he said. 'We see the helicopter going around chasing them. Do you know there was even a couple of gunbattles down the road? There was a kid injured in one of them. I don't go out now much. Before, me and Gracie just used to keep ourselves to ourselves. We did everything together. But I suppose you'd call me a bit of a recluse now.'

When Ron went to see his doctor, she told him that he had cataracts and a damaged retina and referred him to a specialist at the Middlesex Hospital. The specialist examined him and said he needed an operation. The problem was that with delays on the National Health Service it could take weeks if not months before the consultant could attend to him as a public patient. However, if he had the money to go private, then the same consultant could do the operation within a week. Ron asked how much it would cost. The consultant told him he would need more than £2,000 to pay for the treatment. It was everything he had in the bank, his life savings, the money he and Gracie had put away for their retirement. But he was too scared to wait for the NHS to take care of him. The prospect of going to the shops or the post office and not being able to see where he was walking terrified him. He booked the operation and took his money – £2,300 – out of the bank. When I met him it was just a week after the operation. The cataracts had been removed, but the eye surgeon hadn't been able to do anything about the retina. There had been a small improvement in his sight, but he still struggled to focus on faces and was still scared of going out.

Ron was eighty-three years of age, and his entire wealth, the savings he had scraped together over a lifetime, amounted to a little over £2,000. He didn't think there was anything wrong with having so little money at the end of a long working life. But he was bitter that he'd had to hand it over, his small nest egg, to pay for treatment he should have had on the National Health Service.

Ron Roberts was born in 1917 in Black Boy Lane in Tottenham. His father was a veteran of the Boer War, a mounted soldier who'd fought the Afrikaners on the South African veld. When he came home he got a job in a sheet-metal factory and soon after met Ron's mother. She'd been working as a cook at a stately home in Buckinghamshire until she met the returning soldier and became his wife. His father worked for the Lamp Manufacturing Company, making oil lamps for the railways until he retired at the age of seventy. He worked a six-day week but there was little money. Much of what he earned went on the rent of three shillings, four pence a week.

It was a happy childhood. At the weekends his father would sit in the garden and mend the children's shoes and give them haircuts. 'I always remember him sitting there whistling away to himself. Men don't whistle much any more, do they? They were wonderful people, my mum and dad, totally devoted to their children they were.' There were ten children crowded into three bedrooms in the busy lane. The house had one gaslight in the kitchen. All of the other rooms were lit by candles. At times when things were very tight his mother would go to the Prudential and borrow money. This she kept secret from Ron's father. He didn't approve of borrowing. Somehow she managed to keep things going, taking the wages her husband handed over at the end of the week, parcelling out the shillings and pence and keeping creditors from knocking on the door. To this day Ron refuses to borrow money. 'I've never owed a penny in me life. I wouldn't 'ave anything on tick, I pay me way,' he said.

He has vivid memories of the vanished London of the inter-war years. His face comes to life as he talks about it. He remembers buying sweets from the elderly couple who ran Castellanis' sweetshop across the road, the Indian man who came and sold candy floss from a tray, the first Oxo wagon drawn by two cattle with a man giving out free cubes as samples to a wary public, the milkman with his waxed moustache and spotless brass urn from which he dispensed milk with a ladle. There was a local policeman who walked the beat; on summer days he would leave his cape behind a bush in Downhills Park, and Ron and his friends would move it to another bush. 'He used to get mad at us and tell us off, but there was no harm in it. We respected him, we wouldn't 'ave done nothing criminal.'

Like most boys of his class Ron left school in his early teens. He took up a trade as an apprentice carpenter. This was in 1932 and the western world was in the grip of the worst depression in memory. In Germany six million people were unemployed and hyper-inflation had destroyed the value of the mark; in America millions more were destitute and the Democratic presidential challenger, Franklin D. Roosevelt, was advocating the New Deal to rescue the poor. Britain was being governed by a Conservative/Labour national government with the Labour leader Ramsay Mac-Donald as Prime Minister. The previous year the government had been forced to reduce unemployment benefit as part of a series of drastic economies following the collapse of the European banking system. And in Germany, Adolf Hitler was one year away from taking power as Chancellor of the Reich.

By 1939 Ron had married and was the father of a young son. As war approached, he joined the navy ahead of conscription and was trained at Skegness as a signalman. He was sent from there to the navy depot at Lowestoft, where he joined a minesweeping trawler working the east coast from Harwich up to Inverness and back. The minesweepers were a crucial part of the country's coastal defences throughout the war. The ships – mostly trawlers and smaller patrol boats – were in constant danger of attack from German U-boats and aircraft.

There were plenty of near misses. Once he was washed overboard in a storm, another time the boat hit a mine and sank. Luckily they were able to get to the lifeboats in time and everybody was saved. But he lost many friends in the course of the war. It was something you got accustomed to, he said. You knew people could get killed, it was always there in the back of your mind whenever you made friends with someone. That happened with a ship called the *Adonis*, which the Germans sank with twenty men aboard. Ron was supposed to go out with the ship, but his orders were cancelled at the last minute. His brother-in-law Eddie was killed at sea, his ship sunk by torpedoes. 'A lovely guy, Eddie was. He left behind a little daughter. It took me sister a long time to get over that. She married again, but it didn't work out.'

I asked him if he could remember the names of his friends from the navy.

'Not these days, son. I think I'm losing me marbles. With all that's been happening to me, I can't call them back, those names.'

But there was camaraderie?

'Oh yeah. Oh my, yes, there was. We were great friends. Twenty men who didn't know each other from Adam at the start and we ended up trusting each other completely. Out there it could get you down, all the activity and the strain, and we needed each other's company.'

In 1940 he became one of the lucky few to be selected to travel to America to collect ships given to Britain under the Lease-Lend agreement. There was a long train journey across America from New Jersey to Seattle. He has one shining memory of that trip: they were in the west somewhere, travelling across the great open plains, and the train slowed down to move through a crossing. It must have been a place where the drivers were accustomed to cattle straying on to the line. As they passed, Ron looked out of the window and saw a solitary cowboy, sitting on his horse waiting for the carriages to clear so that he might continue on his journey. 'A cowboy! Can you imagine a cowboy? We'd seen 'em at the pictures of course, but you never expected to see one in real life, did you?'

They collected their boat and went down into the Caribbean. There they entered a realm of clear calm water where Ron saw giant turtles, brilliantly coloured sea anemones and bright coral. And once, standing alone at watch, he had seen the shadow of a giant ray emerge from beneath the boat and glide out to the deep. 'Such a sight. My heart missed a beat,' he remembered.

From the Caribbean they crossed the Atlantic to the West African coast. They stopped at Freetown in Sierra Leone. They were working-class boys who'd never set foot outside Britain before. And now they were watching flying fish skim the surface of the water as they approached the vast green mangroves on the African coast. As they prepared to lower the anchor, the boat was surrounded by locals standing in their canoes. He remembered going ashore into the humid tedium of Freetown, a colonial town perched far out on the very edge of the war. 'We threw coins in the water and the natives would dive in and get them. They used to carve these canoes out of wood and balance perfectly in them. If we tried to stand up in the dugouts, we'd just fall over.'

That was his war. A mix of terror and loss, and the most

incredible friendships and memories. Over the years lots of things had departed from him. But the memory of those skinny young men on the deck of that minesweeper he would keep with him always.

On the night the war ended he was sitting on a trawler in Scotland. He doesn't remember any great celebrations, only that the following day a ship was sunk with all hands because a German U-boat captain said he didn't know the war was over. When he came home from the war, London was a battered city. Although he'd been back on leave a few times, he was unprepared for the scale of destruction wrought by Hitler's bombers. 'It was shocking, it really was. My home had been damaged by a bomb which landed close by. It drove kerbstones through the roofs. When I saw what had happened to London, I realized then that the people at home were going through worse than we were. At least we had a gun. They just had to put up with it and bear it.'

On leaving the navy, Ron was given a demob suit and nothing else. 'Homes for heroes they used to say. Homes for heroes! I was lucky to get any bloody work at all.' His wife Alice and young son Roy were living in a rented house in the north London suburb of Hornsey. A second baby was on the way. He changed his trade from carpenter to electrician and went to work for his father's old firm, the Lamp Manufacturing Company. He worked overtime and did odd jobs to earn extra money for his growing family. There were four children in all – two boys and two girls. In many respects his family life was not unlike that of his parents. There was little money, but he and Alice were dedicated to their children. The family *was* their life. Holidays were a week every year at Yarmouth or Broadstairs, the whole family travelling down by train. On weekends he and his two sons went up to King's Cross and watched the trains travelling in and out of London. At work he began to involve himself in trade union activity, joining the Electrical Trades Union and becoming a determined activist. Around the same time he joined the local Labour Party, to which he has remained loyal all his life. 'I wasn't a "one out, all out" merchant in the union. I didn't believe in that. But getting better conditions for the members, that was what interested me. You've gotta stick up for the working man, you know. The lower you are in society, the more you become the victim.'

In the early seventies Alice became ill with cancer and died. He was bereft. Not long afterwards he moved jobs to the Primographic Company, which made nameplates for Rover and Ford cars. It was there that he met his second wife, Gracie, who worked as a secretary for the management. They married in 1977 and stayed working at the firm until it 'downsized' and shifted its base out of London in the mid eighties, a victim of the inexorable decline of British manufacturing. Ron was sixty years of age with no job. He'd been given a redundancy payment of £2,000 but had no pension rights. Without the weekly wage to pay his rent in Hornsey, Ron and Gracie were forced to move out of their flat to the council block on the Caledonian Road.

I asked him if he had ever thought of buying a property.

'Oh no. For us sort of people there wasn't the money to buy properties. We weren't going to get mortgages and that 'cos we weren't making enough money for 'em. Mind you, I don't complain about this flat. We had a good life here for the past twenty-two years. We were very happy here, me and Gracie.'

He got a new job at Sadler's Wells Theatre doing maintenance work and manning the stage door at night. By this time he was well into his seventies. Still, he would work some nights until eleven before shuffling off home to the flat.

But in the middle of the 1990s Gracie became seriously ill with heart trouble and had to have a triple bypass operation. There was difficulty too with her bronchial tubes. She was placed on a course of medication that had the effect of causing water retention in her legs. They swelled up and left her immobile. In 1995, at the age of seventy-eight, Ron finally gave up work to take care of Gracie. 'I had to give up because of her ill health. I had to look after her,' he said.

Life began to slow down and close in on the couple. They left the flat less and less. One winter day she became ill at home, shaking uncontrollably. He took her to hospital. According to Ron, the doctor said Gracie could be treated as an outpatient. She didn't need to be admitted. He explained to the old couple that there was a shortage of beds.

'I asked the nurse in charge how we were going to get home. This was in the evening in November and Gracie was dressed in her nightdress. And the nurse says, "There are plenty of cabs." I says: "I know there are, but you try and find one." I had a hell of a job trying to get her home. That was November 1998. All the following year I was taking her back and forth to the doctor. The last year of her life was the most terrible I could imagine anybody could go through. She didn't get the treatment she deserved. Eventually it got so bad with her legs that she had to be carried up and down the stairs to go to the hospital for outpatient treatment. Every day a health nurse used to come to see her. Then one day I went out shopping and came back to find her lying on the floor with a broken hip. She'd tried to get to the kitchen to get something to eat and had fallen over. That was how I found her.'

Ron couldn't lift his wife from the floor. He telephoned an ambulance that arrived soon after. But it took the paramedics a long time to persuade Gracie to go to hospital. She was terrified. The broken hip was quickly operated on and Gracie transferred to a recovery ward. When he told me this part of the story, the tears began flowing down Ron's cheeks. He recalled how one night the nursing staff had lifted Gracie into her bed; the curtain was drawn and all he could hear was the sound of his wife crying out in pain. It wasn't like her, to cry out. That was why it stayed in his mind so vividly. He went every day and stayed until nine every night, although it was a long bus ride from the Caledonian Road to the Middlesex Hospital.

'I could see Gracie was becoming withdrawn, she was going through so much agony. On the last day she was just staring. She couldn't feed herself. They told me she had an infection. That night I said to her, "I must go, otherwise I won't be able to get home." She threw her arms up in the air. It was the first movement she made that day. She managed to throw one arm around me and I know that Gracie knew she was dying.'

At this point in the conversation, the old man broke down. 'Excuse me,' he said. 'I am sorry.' He started to speak again, with passion, as if he were pleading with me for understanding. 'I didn't know anything life-threatening was happening.' At five o'clock the following morning the telephone rang. It was the hospital. *We're sorry to tell you that your wife has taken a turn for the worse*, they said. He pulled on his clothes and got there in twenty minutes. Gracie was still warm when he arrived. 'Had I known there was anything life-threatening, I'd never have left her. You see, that's what she was doing the night before, she was begging me to stay. That's how she was. She would always have some intimation if someone in her family was having trouble. She was trying to tell me. How can it be that nobody knows she's going to die and she does die? How can that happen?' He missed her every minute of the day, he told me. Sometimes he picks up the photograph album of their life together. He sits with it in his lap, holding the huge magnifying glass, struggling to give clarity to the blurred images in front of him.

On millennium night he sat in and watched the television and went to bed early. Now he had this bother with his eyes, which stopped him going anywhere. Ron had nothing but praise for his children. They had all done well for themselves and they came to see him whenever they could. He struck me as a fiercely independent man, not someone who would want to live in anybody else's house or be shunted into a retirement home. This urge for independence was a feature of elderly life in Britain; the overwhelming majority lived in their own accommodation. But Ron was lonely and bitter; he felt the country he'd served in war, where he'd worked and paid his taxes and raised a good family, had failed to deliver for him when he needed it most. The Health Service that could not fix his eyes in time, the hospital that didn't have a bed for his sick wife on a cold November day, the streets where he was afraid to walk and where angry motorists shouted at him – it was all a long way from the great promise of 1945, of a country that would deliver social and economic justice to all its people. People like Ron knew they had to take what they were given. They did not have power to do anything else.

This wasn't simply a matter of perception. The statistical evidence showed a society that was grievously wanting in its commitment to the old. Consider just two facts: elderly people were twice as likely to live in homes without central heating than those under pension age (this despite their extreme vulnerability to hypothermia); six million people aged sixty-five and older had an annual income of less than £5,090. The benefits they received from the state were enough to get by with as long as they lived frugal lives, but as the charity Help the Aged pointed out: *It indicates a minimum level of income which only really allows for basic living costs; any extras like holidays and leisure activities, house repairs and replacing domestic items can be very hard to afford when living on these levels of income.*

My friend Milton from South Africa had listened to Ron Roberts's story with me. Afterwards, as we drove back to west London, he said he couldn't figure out the British attitude to the elderly. He came from a culture where the old were venerated. Grey hair was a sign of wisdom, you listened to what an old man or woman had to say. When he was growing up, his grandparents lived in the family house. They died in that house and were buried from there. It was the same with most of his friends and neighbours. The new South Africa had one hell of a lot of problems, but in the matter of how people regard the elderly Milton was convinced it could teach Britain a great deal. I've lived in both South Africa and Hong Kong; in these places it was true that the elderly were treated with a degree of reverence that would strike the average British person as unusual. It wasn't just a question of how much old people were given in benefits – in South Africa it is substantially less than the entitlement in the United Kingdom. It was the way in which one society venerated old age, while the other, more affluent and sophisticated, seemed reluctant (a polite definition) to meet its responsibilities.

The office of the charity Help the Aged was situated about ten minutes' drive away from Ron's house, in a small building crammed full of people working hard on behalf of

the elderly. I called in the day after I first met Ron. Tessa
Harding, the policy director, was a soft-spoken woman but
one whose voice vibrated with passion when you asked
about the rights of old people. I mentioned the difference
in attitude from somewhere like South Africa, where in the
black community the elderly were surrounded by their
family in old age, gathered in and taken care of. When it
came to sharing the same house as their children, the British
pensioners were different, she explained. The average
British pensioner, she said, wanted to live an independent
life. It was a deeply ingrained feature of national life and
reflected in the relatively small numbers of old people who
lived in residential homes.

'It is misleading and unfair to say that the family doesn't
care. What you have now is a break up of families because
of housing. There are much greater distances to travel. It is
much more difficult in this society to spend time together.'

Tessa Harding believed the biggest problem was an attitude of mind that only placed value on a person while they
could work. The picture she painted of society's attitude to
the elderly suggested a meretricious, selfish culture. Once
the old had ceased to be valuable work units, they were
shunted aside to become second-class people.

'There is an attitude of mind here which says that when
you retire you are expected to withdraw, to stop being
useful.'

There was something Ron said to me, when he was
talking about his childhood. 'My mum used to always say
she was never happier than when the ten of us were running
around the house. But it's all changed, hasn't it? What's
gone wrong? I always ask myself, what's gone wrong?' And
then he paused to reflect for a moment. An expression of
certainty appeared on his face. 'You know what's missing

now, son? Love, that's it. That's what's missing.' That was part of it, all right. *Love.* It wasn't a word one was used to hearing from people of Ron's generation. They might have felt it, but it was a private word, not to be bandied about in front of strangers. Ron Roberts didn't care for that kind of discretion any longer. He had lost the person he *loved* most. And his country? The one he'd hoped for when he came home from the war had not materialized. And so he was left to think of the country of childhood. That at least had not been lost to him.

# 8. At the Edge of the Union

Why had I come to Castlederg, they wanted to know? Of all places in Northern Ireland? The locals sounded amazed when they heard that someone would want to come back to the place over and again for months. People in Belfast, those I'd worked with in the eighties, would tell me I was off my head. It was a dump. The arse end of nowhere. A bitter, black hole. And on bad days a fair few of the locals might have agreed with you.

Statistically it was pretty close to being the most bombed town in Ulster. There had been thirty murders in the course of the Troubles and who knows how many riots and fights. It was also a poor town, sitting right in the middle of one of the worst unemployment blackspots in the United Kingdom. The land was poor and there was no industry. Apart from a few big shopkeepers, there was nobody you would call 'rich' living in Castlederg.

There may not have been a sink estate for a hundred miles or any high-rise flats, but, believe me, Castlederg was a marginal spot. An excluded place, as much as Govan or Lincoln Green or north Wales. At least in those places you could come up with plans for change; as long as you had the money and the political will, it didn't seem too hard to imagine how the British poor might be helped into a new world. But Castlederg was stuck out on the edge of the Union, physically and psychologically. It was British on the map, but another place entirely in reality. Technically London was the capital. But it might have been Timbuktu for all the relevance Westminster or, for that matter, Belfast had had in the real lives of the people down the years. British governments gave them elections and budgets and new laws. Young men from Leeds and Glasgow and Falmouth had patrolled the streets in the uniform of the British army. The post office boxes bore the imperial crown, and the Union flag fluttered above the police station. In drafty Orange Halls you could listen to them sing 'God Save the Queen', and now and again a local name would feature on the Honours list. A policeman or nurse or community worker.

But, set in the hill country of west Tyrone, with its Irish placenames and its living hatreds, Castlederg did not feel part of anybody's country. Neither Republican Irish nor imperial British. It was a place set apart, miles from the Irish Republic but with its back set safe against British Ulster. The Republic was ten minutes' drive away across raggedy hills fit for sheep and a few hardy cattle. To the east lay the town of Omagh and beyond that again the River Bann and the prosperous fields of mid-Ulster. Further east still was Belfast and then, a world or two away, was London.

I arrived in Castlederg in the middle of winter on a night of rain and wind. It lasted for days, blowing from the Atlantic across Donegal and into Tyrone. It swept down the main street of Castlederg and spat at the windows of the Derg Arms. By the time the summer came I'd developed a fair knowledge of the local geography, including the different routes across the border. The roads of the smugglers and assassins were the same ones used by farmers, tourists and Sunday drivers. I learned where to go for the best view of the hills of Donegal, and where to watch the sun falling over the Sperrin Mountains back in Tyrone. There was no shortage here of quiet places to which I could escape for thinking time. With the ceasefire in place there was little likelihood of stumbling on undercover soldiers or IRA men in the hills. If they were there, I never ran into them. On summer evenings the sun over the Sperrins threw wide blades of light across the valley. But it was light that always seemed tinted with rain, as if a hazy blue filter had been stretched across the face of the sun. The melancholy light of a landscape that held too many secrets. It always reminded me of some lines of Seamus Heaney's:

> Everything ran into water-colour
> The skyline was full up to the lip
> As if the earth were going to brim over.

My favourite place was closer to the town. As you enter Castlederg along the Omagh Road, the ruins of a castle appear on the left-hand side of the road. The ruins stand on the banks of the River Derg, and the land around it has been turned into a public park. Sometimes on summer evenings teenagers go down there to drink cider and shout at each other. Occasionally a police squad car arrives and the kids go quiet. There are cattle grazing in the field alongside the river and the sandy bank is stippled with their hoof marks.

Sammy Walls, who runs the Derg Arms, told me the fishing on the river was some of the best in the country. You can see the river and castle from the back bedrooms of the Arms. There were big brown trout and sea trout as well, running up from the Atlantic, he said. If you hung around the riverbank long enough you could see heron and otters. And in the dusk, with the mayfly rising and fish on the bite, I could close my eyes and try to imagine this place as it might have been before the long siege, where a man could fish without listening for other sounds besides the water and cattle. Not then the ear cocked for the sound of riders and clinking armour, or in modern times the boots running swiftly across grass or the bullet clicking into the chamber.

The castle from which the town takes its name was built by an English planter, Sir John Davies, in 1609. Davies was a gentleman soldier who served as solicitor-general in Ireland and, in keeping with the views of his contemporaries, regarded the native Irish as barbarous heathens. By the time he arrived, the area around Castlederg had experienced relentless warfare and a policy of scorched earth courtesy of the invading English. That is not to say that the native chieftains were enlightened and kind rulers; but they did have the advantage of being native and were tolerated by the people. Being dragged into a union with England, to live under English lords and an English queen, was a different prospect. However, when confronted with the threat of foreign domination, the chiefs did not unite. Instead they indulged in the ancient tradition of fighting each other. Alliances were formed and discarded, armies raised and battles fought, but the English never went away. There were moments of unity. The principal chiefly family in Tyrone, the O'Neills, led an Irish army to defeat at Kinsale in County Cork, having made an heroic march through the country in the middle of winter. Soon afterwards the majority of the old Irish aristocracy, defeated and exhausted, set sail for Europe from a place just a few miles down the road from Castlederg.

The town's history is one of unending siege. The sense of living among untrustworthy neighbours can be detected in the letters and diaries of the colonists from the earliest days of the plantation. The historian Roy Foster quotes one of Elizabeth's commanders describing the native Irish as 'servile, crafty and inquisitive after news, the symptoms of a conquered nation'. If you were to add to that the terms 'dirty' and 'savage', you would have some idea of the psychology that would later underpin Loyalist attitudes to their Catholic neighbours.

When the native Irish rose up in 1641, they struck at settlements across Ulster. Irish forces under Sir Phelim O'Neill attacked the castle. Today you can see the gaps in the wall where cannon hammered away at the granite. There were massacres that passed into Protestant folklore. The isolated settler community was terror struck. Quoting a contemporary account, Roy Foster describes what happened: 'The Irish servant which overnight was undressing his master in Duty, the next morning was stripping master and mistress with a too officious tyranny.' Settlers and their families were wiped out as neighbour descended on neighbour in a blood frenzy that would ultimately claim around 4,000 lives. The retaliation against the Catholics claimed as many lives again. The effect on the psyches of the planter and the defeated native proved irredeemably destructive. What slender trust that had existed there before was now entirely gone.

In Castlederg the siege was set in stone. History would later produce Cromwell, William of Orange, Robert Emmet and the rebellion of 1798, the Young Irelanders, the Fenians, the 1916 rising and the Anglo-Irish war. And after that came the border and seventy years of intermittent killing. The last thirty had only been the latest instalment in a long-running tragedy. It would take 350 years before the descendants of planter and native would contemplate a shared future.

As it happened, I arrived in town just as the business of peacemaking was getting under way in earnest in distant

Belfast. For the first time in generations a British government had committed itself wholeheartedly to forging a
peace in Ulster. Tony Blair and Mo Mowlam were a duo
unlike anything ever before seen in Ulster. There was
energy in the air. Things were moving. The Labour government had come to power promising to restart the peace
process in Northern Ireland. It wasn't an issue that won
votes, but Blair was a politician who spoke as if he had a
deep moral conviction. Ireland would be sorted out because
it was the right thing to do. And in the South there was a
similar determination. Abandoning the territorial claim to
the North was firmly on the agenda. To a generation that
had grown up in a modernizing, increasingly secular republic, the pieties of the past no longer seemed so precious. If
there could be justice for Northern Nationalists, then we
were less concerned with flags and symbols and old claims
to own this or that. More than anything we wanted to be
rid of the killing. It diminished all of us on the island, it
represented an image of Irishness we felt we'd long out-
grown: the Brit-hating gunman was to most of us a shame-
inducing anachronism.

Things were moving, and it was hard for the Irish exile
watching from Britain to avoid feeling a sense of excitement.
I watched the appointment of David Trimble and Seamus
Mallon as First Minister and Deputy First Minister and
pinched myself. After the long dialogue of the deaf, the
politicians were actually working with each other! Cease-
fires, powersharing, Sinn Féin talking to Unionists. It was
happening in front of me and I struggled to believe it. But
I'd lived long enough in Northern Ireland to have a little
circumspection. The peace was being made in Belfast and
London, but how would it play in the towns and villages of
Ulster, in somewhere like Castlederg? I had boldly told my

friends in Belfast how I wanted to 'get under the skin' of Castlederg. An appalling cliché, of course, and a declaration of the impossible. No outsider gets under the skin of a town like Castlederg. How does an interloper understand a place where death is the patient neighbour who smiles and salutes and whispers your movements to a killer and then attends your funeral? Whose skin would I get under?

In the end it happened the other way around. Castlederg got under my skin. It caught hold of my liberal pieties and shook them hard. I had come from London, full of the rhetoric of hope. A Southern Irishman at ease with the English. Peace was within our grasp. A lasting peace. A peace with justice. A peace based on recognizing the validity of each tradition. I didn't need Tony Blair to give me those lines – I'd been writing them myself for years.

'Peace my arse,' the big fellow had said on my first night in Castlederg. 'What about them boys lying six feet under out on the Omagh road? Go and tell them about peace.'

I met him in the bar of the Derg Arms – a tall, broad-shouldered man with red cheeks and curly, fair hair. It was an hour before closing time and I'd come in for a nightcap. He was drinking with a couple of local men, one of whom had been filling me in on the history of the place. He was drunk, and he looked at me with suspicion.

'What's your name, then?' he asked.

'Fergal,' I replied.

'Fergal,' he said. 'Isn't that the queer name to have in a pub like this.'

It wasn't a question but a straightforward statement of fact. My name was as Fenian as they come. Not as common as Sean or Seamus or Pat – but straight out of the Irish all the same. And the accent in which it was announced was three hundred miles to the south of Castlederg. The questioner was right to be surprised. Southern boys with fine broad Fenian names were a rare species in the late-night drink-time of the Derg Arms.

After the big fellow's intervention I was ready to head somewhere else. But he bought me a drink and urged me to stay. And then he took my hand in his. The intimacy was unsettling. It was a big, broad, rough hand. It might as easily punch me through the wall as pay for a drink. He squeezed it tight and began to recite a story from his time in the Ulster Defence Regiment. There was a fellah locally whom they all knew was in the Provos, he said. A nasty bad fucker who'd set up a friend of his for murder. Then one night there was a bomb at this boy's house. It hadn't exploded and the disposal squad were on their way. The big fellow and his patrol were sent down as well. They went in to get the family out. He said the man of the house wouldn't talk to him at all. Except near the end, when everyone was out. Then your man starts to abuse them, calling them Loyalist bastards. That's what he said and they were in there saving his family.

While he was telling the story, the grip on my hand was slowly loosened, but he never let it go entirely. He said the house was the dirtiest he was ever in. 'Fuck me, but the smell of pish in that place was something wicked. I never smelt the like of it,' he said. 'What do ye think of that, Fergal?' He stretched the vowels of the name and smiled.

'Sounds rough, all right,' I said. Had I been there on my own I might have been frightened. The fear that goes with not knowing who exactly you are talking to, what they belong to and where the conversation is headed. Would it move from local loathing into a more generalized blast at my tribe? And would others join in and wait outside after?

But the others were friendly and Sammy behind the bar

would have made sure things didn't get out of hand. And, drunk as he was, the big fellow was no Shankill Road hard man who might shake my hand and then slit my Fenian throat. There was a tradition of hospitality in this house. And the other drinkers – teachers and businessmen – made a point of saying how they were sick of politics. I sensed they were a bit embarrassed by the big fellow. They wanted to talk about the trips they made to the South and the games of golf they played across in Donegal. 'Nobody here gives a shite about politics. If it wasn't for a few lunatics making money out of the whole thing, sure there'd be no troubles at all,' said one of them. It is the kind of talk that is half true and half false. The talk of men and women who want a quiet life.

The big fellow eventually let go of my hand and ordered another round of drinks. He was well drunk and starting to slur. There was bitterness in his tone. The Ulster Defence Regiment to which he belonged was gone. He had buried friends who were killed for wearing the uniform. And now what did they have? The Royal Irish Regiment, the UDR dead and buried. And were the Sinn Féiners happy with the new crowd? The fuck they were. Always complaining. Roy had long since given up his role as an armed defender of the Union. Though he still wore the Sash and still marched on the 12th of July, he was a businessman these days and wished like everybody else that the Troubles would go away.

The way the big fellow described things, Castlederg was a place where trust and fellowship were in short supply across the sectarian divide. There was an old subtext – I'd encountered it so often in Ulster – that divided the Catholic population into 'good' Catholics and 'bad' Catholics. And then there was another, more unsettling category: the Bad

Catholics whom you mistook for Good Catholics until it was too late.

One or the other drinkers in the Derg Arms told me the story of Josie Connolly. Josie was a local Catholic boy who'd been blown up by his own bomb in 1989. Local Nationalists said he was a lovely lad. Sensitive and quiet. He'd been born in Glasgow and came back to live in Castlederg with his family. Even the Protestants admit they were shocked when Josie's name was broadcast on the radio news bulletin. An IRA man? Him, a lad that always smiled at you and said hello, a good fellow to pass the time of day with. Josie was working for the same building firm as an RUC reservist. They worked on the same jobs and, according to the Protestant version of things, the reservist used to share his lunch with Josie. But Josie was watching his workmate. He noted what time he left work and what route he used. And he noted his address. Late one February night, Josie turned up outside his workmate's home with a bomb and a pistol. He was halfway through planting the bomb when it exploded. Josie Connolly died in hospital the following night. 'And he working with the man he was trying to kill. Sitting in the cab with him and sharing his food with him. How could you trust the likes of that?' the teller of the story asked. The pistol they'd found on Josie had been used to kill two other UDR men. When he was buried, Gerry Adams and Martin McGuinness went to the funeral. Adams said his death was a 'terrible indictment' of the state. Whatever that meant.

And now the big fellow and the rest of Castlederg's Protestants were being asked to contemplate a government in which Gerry Adams and Martin McGuinness could be ministers. Men whom the big fellow suspected of having murdered his friends were being released from prison. He was angry, confused and fearful. The long war had brought a lot of pain, but there was a certainty about everybody's role. You knew where you stood. Trust your friends and family, and keep a close eye on the other side. I'm not saying he didn't welcome the peace. It was more a question of how he felt about the price being paid for that peace. Talking to Castlederg's Protestants, I gradually had the sense that the deal with Sinn Féin was viewed as a defeat. However much their leaders might dress it up, they sensed that the old enemy had breached the castle walls again and this time they wouldn't be pushed back. They'd done it with negotiations and smiles and press conferences. The Protestants had heard a British Prime Minister declare to the world that Britain had no 'selfish or strategic' interest in holding on to Ulster. No more important sentence had been uttered since Gladstone's first Home Rule Bill over a century before. Here was a place that Margaret Thatcher had once declared 'as British as Finchley'. Barely ten years later her successor John Major was announcing what little interest the British people had in holding on to it.

And then there was the example of the Scots. Most of the Protestants living around Castlederg were of Scottish extraction. Across the water their kith and kin were moving inexorably towards independence. In the last years of the British century constitutional change was at the top of the political agenda. *No selfish or strategic interest.* It was words like these, the sense of constitutional upheaval and the old suspicion of British motives, so long an integral part of the Unionist psyche, that convinced the big fellow and many of his friends that the rug was being pulled slowly out from under them.

From the Derg Arms up to the Catholic end of town it is a walk of about three minutes. The young people who riot here in the marching season and on weekend nights

cover the distance in much quicker time. If you don't want
a kicking, you avoid the enemy's end of town or you make
sure you have a quick pair of legs. The taunting is tribal and
intimate. Is it all that different from youth gangs in London
or Leeds? Not that much, I suspect. The immediate causes
were similar: boredom and drink and shrunken horizons.
The difference, of course, was in the history. History gave
them grievance, all right. It also gave them an alibi. Every
bigoted shout from one side or the other could be dignified
by history. Standing up for their rights, protecting their
traditions, righting the ancient wrong.

They could watch the life of the streets from the observation
tower of the RUC station at the top of the town. The
cameras scanned the streets below in black and white, peeking down laneways and across rooftops. The station was
bombed repeatedly by the IRA and several of its officers
were murdered in the Troubles. In the halfway house of
the ceasefire – a war suspended, not ended – the officers
were still careful about their movements. But men were
starting to patrol without flak jackets and stopping to pass
the time of day with people on the street.

Right across the road from the police station is the Catholic church and beyond is a Nationalist estate. As you walk
up main street, you pass the shop where Olven Kilpatrick
was murdered in 1977. The big fellow knew Olven. Everybody who lived in Castlederg knew Olven. He owned the
shoe shop and lived on Prospect Terrace not far from the
main street with his wife and two children. Olven had been
a part-time member of the UDR and a member of a local
Orange lodge. On a January morning two IRA men walked
straight in and shot him. They left behind a bomb in a
shoebox. That was to catch the army and police when they

arrived to investigate the shooting. The bomb went off and injured two policemen. There was a fire and Olven's body couldn't be retrieved until the fire brigade arrived and stopped the flames. A Protestant woman told me Olven had seen a couple of known IRA men walking up and down outside his shop the day before he was killed. But he thought they were just trying to put the wind up him. He knew the Provos would have him on a death list, but he stayed in the UDR.

Olven had belonged to the Castlederg First Presbyterian Church. Over the years the church had lost eight members in IRA attacks, all of them members of the security forces. Men like William Bogle, shot dead as he was watching over his three infant sons while his wife was in the post office. The Troubles followed the Bogles like a bad spell: in 1993 William Bogle's mother died of a heart attack after an IRA bomb exploded in Castlederg. Bogle, Rankin, Pollock, Monteith, Sproule, Clarke, Elliot, Kerrigan, Finley, Darcy: names on headstones in country churchyards. The Protestant dead of Castlederg.

Darcy. It was that last name that had brought me to Castlederg ten years ago on my first visit. Michael Darcy. He was one of the men shot dead with the pistol found on Josie Connolly's body. Darcy was eight years older than Connolly. He was murdered seven months before the IRA man blew himself up. Did Josie pull the trigger himself? We will never know. If he didn't, he will have known the man who did. And he would surely have celebrated Michael Darcy's death.

To the Protestants, a man like Josie Connolly was a terrorist, pure and simple. But up in Nationalist Castlederg, in a house whose gable wall is decorated with the images of dead IRA men, Paddy Devlin bridles at the word *terrorist*.

He lives in a neat council estate on one of the roads leading to Donegal. The graffiti eulogizes the IRA and warns the police to keep out. The orange, white and green of the Irish tricolour is painted on a wall near the entrance. But it's low-key stuff compared to the Republican estates of Belfast or Derry. Nor does it feel remotely threatening. This is still a rural area. Here the presence of the IRA in the neighbourhood remains a powerful deterrent to the hoods and drug dealers who have set up shop in the urban estates.

Paddy Devlin had a warm welcome for me. He had a fondness for Kerry where my father's people came from, and he knew my uncle's plays and his dedication to the Irish language. Paddy was wheelchair-bound because of an accident several years before. He was separated from his wife, and his two sons and a daughter shared the house with him. Paddy was a devoted activist for the rights of the disabled and a familiar sight buzzing along the roads of Castlederg on his motorized tricycle. There was a lot of warmth in the man and a sadness I never really understood. Doubtless he would say that was because I had grown up in a safe place, sure of my rights. There were times when we spoke when tears came into Paddy's eyes. He might be talking about the traditions and culture of the native Irish or the men who died in a long-forgotten rebellion. And then his eyes would start to sparkle and his voice tremble.

When we met he insisted on speaking in Irish for the first few minutes of the conversation. Paddy was making a point – about his identity and mine, about what we shared and what made us different from the English. I'd been given his name by a local Sinn Féin member. Paddy was a solid Republican, he said, and a man who could fill me in on Castlederg life in the last years of the twentieth century. But Paddy didn't just want to talk about the twentieth century.

Over a few nights and several whiskeys he spoke of many
centuries. The plantation, the rebellions, the famine. I had
grown up listening to these stories at school. Seven hundred
years of English treachery, the brave men of 1916. Identity
seemed to be his obsession. Who he was, who we all were.
The map said he lived in the United Kingdom of Great
Britain and Northern Ireland. But Paddy belonged somewhere else. The border enraged him, it was like a line
chiselled around his personal horizon. He did remember a
time when Protestants and Catholics worked in the fields
together. They gathered the harvest, picked potatoes and
shared milk from their cattle. But the rural calm was nothing
more than a lid on a slowly boiling pot. He could remember
the B-Specials roadblocks, the landscape Heaney described
so memorably in 'The Ministry of Fear':

What's your name, driver?

Seamus.

*Seamus?*

'We lost our sense of identity and in that way we were
dispossessed,' said Paddy. 'They were put up into the mountains, our people. The landlords came over and they had
their big houses and tenants. They came over from Scotland
and the north of England.' *They* and *Them*. The oppressive
*other*. It was in literal terms all true. I remember a Protestant
saying to me in Castlederg, 'Our big mistake was to drive
them up to the high ground. They've been plaguing us
from there ever since.' He was joking, but in Castlederg a
joke like that invariably shelters a hard truth. And if you
thought that was all four hundred years ago, something
people should long ago have forgotten or got over, then
you didn't understand Paddy Devlin or the big fellow or
the nature of memory in a place like Castlederg.

It was hard to quibble over facts. Paddy knew his history.

But I felt he didn't much care for the other man's determination to be British or what that Britishness might mean to him. When I listened to him talk about the local Protestants, he sounded generous. When I read his remarks in transcript, they sounded patronizing. I suspect a Castlederg Protestant would see them as arrogant: 'There will always be a place for the Protestant. I don't know whether I would describe the Protestants as British. But they must be given the space to examine who they are and come to terms with the major change in the status quo that they have known for the last seventy-five years.'

I butted in and asked him if he respected their right to see themselves as British?

'Of course. Of course.' And then he talked about the diversity of culture and national identity. Lurking at the heart of all this, I suspect, was a belief that the British Protestants of Castlederg would someday assimilate. 'British is not really an identity as such . . . there's a lot of gaps in it, a lot of gaps. But we must allow them time to adjust and come to terms with who they are and where they want to go.'

It wasn't that Paddy was a sectarian bigot. And he had a candour you'd struggle to find among a lot of Ulster's mainstream politicians. But he had anger about the past, and he relished an idea of Irish identity that many people of my generation had long since abandoned.

As a Southerner who now lived a comfortable middle-class life in Britain, I was in a poor position to empathize with him. My world and his, our ideas of what it meant to be Irish and our attitudes to the English, were a long way apart. Would I have been different if I'd been born in Castlederg and harassed at UDR checkpoints, if my cultural environment was determined by trying to see the difference between me and *them*? Could I have been an IRA man instead of a pious apostle of peace? Quite easily, I'm sure. All of the dead men and boys of Castlederg believed their identity was something worth fighting for.

Forget the nonsense you've read and heard about the war being rooted in money. A man didn't wear a UDR uniform and face the everyday possibility of assassination for the money. Nor did IRA men and women risk death or jail, and become willing to take the lives of others, for the sake of money. A few people got rich from the Troubles. But they were so few that the security experts in Northern Ireland could probably name them all for you.

When I grew up, the fight for self-determination was something we hadn't had to consider for more than seventy years. I guess I belong to what Paddy dismissively called the 'Dublin 4 Set'. For that, read the middle-class supporters of a liberal, post-nationalist, secular Irish identity. We might occasionally flinch when an English voice said something patronizing or when some comedian cracked a joke about the Irish. But we liked to think of ourselves as being 'beyond all that'. Not for us the Ireland of rebel hearts and devout prayers. I think men like Paddy regarded us as spoiled. And in a way he was right. My generation of middle-class Southerners had never had to fight for anything. The idea that in this day and age anybody in these islands of the north Atlantic should feel justified in killing for political reasons struck me as perverse. Though he never said it, I knew Paddy had me marked down as grievously mistaken.

In Paddy's world boys like Josie Connolly who died trying to kill their neighbours were heroic figures. I asked him if he was proud of the IRA. 'Yes. Because if it were not for the IRA, I think things could have been a hell of a lot worse for the Nationalist community . . . they have their faults and they are many . . . but were it not for them, I believe the consequences could have been a lot worse.' Paddy Devlin shared one conviction with the big fellow. He believed that history had turned in the Nationalists' favour. There would be a united Ireland, an end to the United Kingdom in his lifetime. He had listened to John Major's Downing Street Declaration and taken exactly the same message as the big fellow.

Paddy never said this to me, but I'd had enough conversations with Nationalists to gauge the general expectation. The peace process would stumble along. If the Assembly could be made to work, then power would be drained away bit by bit from the British state. The 'Irish' dimension would grow with Protestants drawn inexorably into ever closer contact with the Republic. Sooner or later they would realize they were better off joining the rest of the island in political union. If it didn't work out – and a lot of the men and women I spoke to had the gravest doubts – the Brits would eventually get fed up with the Protestants and declare their intention to withdraw. And the Protestants would be so disgusted that they'd make their accommodation with Dublin. Was it pipe dreaming? I think the Nationalists were pretty good judges of the long-term British interest in Northern Ireland; but I was convinced they would be mistaken to think the Protestants might give up without a fight. And that ultimately is what kept the British government in Northern Ireland. It had nothing to do with any conviction that the Protestants were as British as Londoners, but rather with the fear of a nasty civil war on London's doorstep. And as long as that fear remained, the commitment to keeping Ulster British would not be abandoned.

★

Up at the top of the town where there were three Catholic bars close to each other, the RUC riot squad was drawn up in lines on either side of the road. Ahead of me the bandsmen of the Castlederg Young Loyalists were marching towards their 11th night bonfire. Tonight they wore football t-shirts, denims, sneakers. A gang of working-class kids like any you might see in London or Glasgow or Dublin. Tomorrow – the 12th of July – they would don the toy soldier uniform of a Loyalist marching band and join bands from all over Tyrone at a parade in Sion Mills, about fifteen minutes away.

The atmosphere on the way out was good humoured. I am an inveterate coward in these situations, always fearing that someone will spot my Southern accent and become aggressive. It has happened once or twice. In Portadown, the capital city of Ulster bigotry, a Loyalist bandsman overheard me talking to a policeman. He walked up to the two of us and politely informed me that the only place for Fenians like me was on top of a bonfire with the priests. I became a little paranoid at Loyalist demonstrations after that, restricting my conversation to the bare minimum, choked grunts of assent or dissent. But by now many of the Castlederg marchers knew who I was. And none of them seemed to hold the fact of my Southern papishness against me.

I was walking with Derek Hussey, the local Ulster Unionist Party Assemblyman, who was a solid supporter of David Trimble. Derek had only just been elected to the Assembly, the body from which a new power-sharing executive would be created. He was a short, stocky man, with red hair, a beard and piercing green eyes. There was an intensity about him and a streetwiseness that set him apart from many of the rural Unionist politicians I'd known in the past. Maybe it came from making his living as a publican and nightclub owner. I had the strong sense that Derek Hussey was not a man I'd want to tangle with at closing time. His great passion in life apart from politics was country and western music. Acts like Daniel O'Donnell and Brian Coll and the Buckaroos enjoyed a huge popular following among both communities. This was the music of frontier land. There was a time when Derek toured the dancehalls of Ulster with his own country band. He still played the guitar in the pub and hosted 'Davy Crockett' nights, when his customers would come dressed in cowboy clothes. Local legend claims that Davy Crockett's family emigrated to the States from Castlederg. To leave Castlederg and end up at the Alamo! Poor old Davy Crockett, a martyr to bad choices.

In the Assembly elections a majority of Castlederg Protestants had chosen to follow Trimble's path of moderation by voting for Derek Hussey. But the 11th night marchers were a different proposition. They had little time for Trimble. They were mostly young and many were unemployed. They were the children of the Loyalist housing estates and small farms around Castlederg. They were not a political force, but they'd latched on to the rhetoric of an older Unionism and made it their own. No Surrender. No Popery. In the long run they wouldn't make a blind bit of difference to the peace process as long as the politicians at the top held the Agreement together. It was only in times of doubt, when men like Derek Hussey wavered and seemed under pressure from the Unionist extremes, or when the IRA or one of their offshoots committed an atrocity, that these young people came into their own. In estates across Ulster they could riot and burn cars and stone the police. Television news broadcasts would speak darkly of an Ulster in crisis. The army's Spearhead Battalion would be put on standby. And it would last a few days, occasionally even a few weeks, before fizzling out.

But in the small life of a town they had the capacity to impose fear. A local Nationalist running into this mob when they were tanked up could expect a bad beating. (The opposite was also true. The Loyalist bandsman walking home from practice was rightly wary of the treatment he could expect from a gang of Catholic youths.) When the band marched up the street on the 11th night, most of the Catholics stayed indoors. I could see a few faces peering from the upstairs windows of the Catholic businesses. The riot squad was standing ready to keep neighbours from beating the daylights out of neighbours.

Most of the youngsters had known Derek Hussey for years. He'd been a founder member of the flute band and had taught many of them in the local Protestant school. And yet now he was standing foursquare behind David Trimble. Now he was someone willing to do a deal with the IRA, who had killed their friends and his. I broke away from Derek for a few minutes to watch the tail-end of the parade. Very often it was the stragglers on such marches who provoked trouble. As I stood on the corner, a man with thick glasses and curly black hair came over. 'I see you're hangin' about with Hussey, then,' he said. I told him my story. How I wanted to understand what the Protestants were going through now that a peace deal was in the making. 'That Hussey boy,' he said, 'that fellah is after selling out everything we believed in. If the men that were murdered by the IRA could see him now, they'd be turning in their graves. You tell him that. Tell him I said that.' I asked for his name, so that I could pass on the message. But he walked off quickly in the direction of the band.

I rejoined Derek, who said he was staying with the march all the way to the bonfire site. This took some courage. When I asked him why he'd come, he answered with a note of exasperation. 'Because it's my right. I have always come and I always will come.'

We reached the bonfire site at dusk. By now many of the crowd were drunk. I stuck close to Derek and kept my mouth shut. The flag of the Irish Republic fluttered on top of the great bonfire – on top of tables and chairs and boxes and tractor tyres and every bit of household scrap you could imagine. A couple of men stepped out of the crowd with flaming torches and walked to the base of the structure. 'Fuck Trimble,' somebody close to me shouted. 'Fuckin' traitor,' someone else mumbled. This last shred of abuse was directed at Derek. If he heard it, he did not look around. Arguing among drunks at an 11th night bonfire would have been foolish. The men thrust their torches into the bonfire and up it went. The dry timber exploded and flames shot out in all directions as the crowd cheered. Sparks flew out over the heads of the drinkers. By the time the flames reached the tricolour, the cheering had become a frenzy.

And all the time the band hammered out the blood and thunder tunes of a thousand 11th nights; the same noise that had rattled the windows of British Prime Ministers for generations. I had heard it many times before in towns and villages across Ulster. But now it was not the frightening roar of a defiant mass. Mr Blair would not worry about the curses that rained down on him here or at any of the other drunken bonfires on this 11th night. Across in Drumcree, an hour's drive away, they were squaring up to fight with the army and police, but even that confrontation would soon fizzle out, destroyed by a petrol bomb hurled through the window of a Catholic house.

The bonfire blazed away and then the band turned to march back into town. There were a few more mutterings near Derek Hussey, but again he ignored them. As we

reached the Catholic bars, the band belted their drums and
the shouts grew louder. I noticed that a few people had
gathered in the doorway of a Catholic pub. A youngster of
about ten was standing just outside the door. A band
member pushed the boy as he passed. His father jumped
out to confront the bandsman and was immediately shoved
back into the doorway by the riot squad. There were curses
and blows. 'Fuck the Pope,' somebody shouted into my
face. It was over in seconds. Why on earth were they
standing out there? I asked myself. On this night of all
nights. Why? Perhaps to say 'We are not afraid.' Or to say
'This is our end and don't you forget it.' Whatever con-
fusion I had, I suspect the bandsmen understood it all
completely. This was the kind of incident that was played
out every marching season. The drink and the anger. The
shout and the scuffle. It meant nothing and it meant everything. Tony Blair would never hear about this; but it would
be remembered in Castlederg, stored up until the chance
presented itself for a settling of scores. The last thing I
saw that night was Derek Hussey standing in the street
surrounded by a group of angry men. They were arguing
and gesticulating.

After a while the men seemed to tire of the argument.
They turned and walked away and left Derek to his
thoughts. In the last couple of years Derek had been making
some big choices himself. Nationalists told me that in the
past he'd been an uncompromising Loyalist. They pointed
to his role in the flute band and his devotion to the Orange
Order. His stance in support of Trimble was something
they, and his old Loyalist friends, found hard to understand.
I liked the man a lot. It was hard not to, with his quick wit
and his courage and his willingness to try to see the other
side's point of view. Over the course of many weeks, I

tried to fathom what it was that had turned Derek into a moderate. A cynic would have said that it was political ambition. He saw that Trimble was going to be First Minister and he fancied his chances as a cabinet minister. Could it have been that the man on the street corner was right: Hussey had sold out on his friends and what he believed in for the sake of power? But nothing could have been more wrong. I found out the truth of the matter quite by accident, listening to the story of an old woman and her dead son.

# 9. Motherland

If you walk swiftly, it will take you around ten minutes to go from Derek Hussey's pub down to where Kathleen Darcy lives. Kathleen is in her seventies and disabled. Not long before I came back to see her she'd been diagnosed with bowel cancer. (It would kill her within the year.) In the days when I lived in Belfast I'd reported the death of her son Michael Darcy for the Irish broadcasting station, Radio Telefís Éireann. It was the gun found on Josie Connolly, the building worker killed by his own bomb, that had been used to kill Michael.

Inside the door of her home Kathleen had hung a drawing of her son. It was drawn from a photograph of him in his UDR uniform, taken some time in the year before his death. The dead son smiled down at the visitors who passed in and out of her council house. Mostly they were neighbours or health care workers. They knew the facts of Michael's death and had long ago stopped asking questions. He was just the face in the drawing on the wall, smiling and dead, every day. Michael Darcy, aged twenty-eight, murdered by the Provisional IRA in February 1988. I had reported many murders in Ulster, but the memory of that old widow losing her only son had stuck with me more than any of the others. 'Wee Mikey' she used to call him, with the tears filling her eyes. Kathleen Darcy had said I should come back and see her some time. 'Come back when you've time. It takes a wee while to tell the whole story,' she'd said. And I, the reporter who rushed in and out of people's lives, shrinking their tragedies into three-minute packages, made a mental promise that I would.

The Nationalists I'd spoken to said Michael Darcy was a sectarian bigot. Nobody would go on the record, but they claimed he'd harassed people at roadblocks and even attacked a Catholic church late one night. I knew the police had once wanted to question him in connection with an assault on a Catholic youth, and that Kathleen had persuaded them her son couldn't possibly have been involved.

It wasn't difficult to believe that a UDR man had given Catholics a hard time at checkpoints. There had been enough convictions of UDR men for extreme Loyalist activities to engender deep Nationalist suspicion of the force. I fell foul of them myself one Christmas. Travelling back from the South, my car packed with presents, I was stopped on the road outside Belfast. The soldiers kept my wife and myself for an hour while they unwrapped every one of our presents, laughing to each other about the delay they were causing. When they finished, they refused to stow away the presents and luggage. And so I smiled and thanked them and packed the stuff away myself. That was an easy gesture for me. I had no history with these boys. They were not my neighbours. And I had not grown up in their world, or learned its humiliations and anger.

Had I been a local Catholic, though, how would I have reacted? How would they have treated me? Curses and blows maybe? As I was an obviously middle-class Southerner, they had to be more wary with me. They stuck to the rules. They just inflicted as much annoyance as they legally could.

Kathleen Darcy didn't believe the stories of harassment. Michael had been there to serve his country. He never did anyone any wrong, though there was a few around Castlederg that well deserved some trouble, she said.

The intervening years had been hard on Kathleen. Her health had failed badly and she lived with a daunting litany of illness. She had angina, cataracts, arthritis. And now there was word from the hospital that she'd developed cancer of the bowel. When we met she looked a great deal older and more frail than I remembered. She was in the kitchen making toast when I called. I asked her whether she remembered me, and after some uncertainty she let on that she did.

'Ach, of course I do. How are ye? Will ye have a cup of tea?' And then she pointed to the little pile of tablets on the table. One for each of her ailments. 'I'm right weak now, I can tell ye. I'm on me last legs. The doctor says I'm not to move around at all. But sure what kind of life is that? Where would you be going, just trapped in here all day long? Would you answer me that?'

Her house was tiny. A bedroom, a sitting room, a kitchen and a toilet. Everywhere you looked there were paintings of statuettes of horses. They were Kathleen's big thing. Horses of every size and colour. Kathleen's house was set in a line that faced the hall where the flute band practised. Her son had been one of the founders of the band, 'The Castlederg Young Loyalists'. Now as she watched the evenings lengthen, Kathleen Darcy could hear the fifes and drums, and the feet stamping on wood as the Young Loyalists limbered up for the marching season.

We drank tea and she told me more about her health. There were some local women who looked in on her and a nurse who was very decent. And there was Derek Hussey, a friend of Michael who came every few days to see if she was all right. Derek had been in the flute band with Mikey and now he was running for politics with the Ulster Unionist Party. Derek was a lovely man, she said. But why he was getting involved in that bloody politics she couldn't understand. I ended up staying there for several hours. I asked the occasional question but mostly just listened. Kathleen Darcy's story was not the one I had been conditioned to expect. I had thought I'd covered every permutation of the Ulster story. The grieving family member who speaks of their anger and sorrow, who declares forgiveness or says they will never forgive, who believes there can be peace or says all the politics is just nonsense. I had them all boiled down to the expected; but Kathleen's was unlike any story I'd ever heard in Northern Ireland. It was a story about the Troubles. But it was also a parable about the nature of identity, about society and family and about belonging. I would learn that Kathleen Darcy and her boy were people of the margins; they wanted to belong and in the end that human longing brought them desolation. 'Where will I start?' she asked. I said: 'Start at the very beginning.'

Kathleen Darcy went back to her roots. Her mother, she said, had come up from the Free State after getting pregnant by a man down there. In those days a girl would often take flight like that, unable to face the shame of a bastard child. One evening two local lads were passing by the river when they heard a woman crying by the bank. They went down and found Kathleen's mother. She was heavy with child and frantic for the want of shelter and food. One of the men took her in and she ended up staying on in Castlederg. Somewhere along the way she met Kathleen's father, a local Protestant who'd served in the army and the B-Specials. She married him, but after giving birth to six children she died at the age of forty-six. That was how it was in those days, said Kathleen. Her father was fond of drink and he took up with another woman who had several children of her own. There was little money around, and Kathleen and her brother Billy were sent out to work for local farmers. In those days they still held hiring fairs in rural towns, north and south of the border. 'You were hired out for about a pound a month or so. We used to go gathering spuds and one thing or another, you know. God save us, the life we had. To get extra money we used to go around collecting empty stout bottles and collect the returns on them. There was no carrying on, though. If Sergeant Flanagan ever caught you at anything, he'd just wallop you one right across the face. And if you went home and said he'd hit you, you got another beating.'

Kathleen was often beaten by her father. 'He was a devil by times,' she said. Once he knocked her flying across the room and she landed under a table, breaking her collarbone. In those days doctors patched up the injuries caused by domestic violence and sent the children home. It was a world before social workers and care orders, and Kathleen Darcy survived on her wits.

At the age of sixteen she took off for London. Half of Ireland was heading for London in those days. After the war and in the grip of recession, there were few jobs, North or South. Kathleen's first job was as a cleaner. It was a strange building full of one-room flats occupied by single women. It took Kathleen several weeks to figure out she'd taken a job as housekeeper in a brothel. She still laughs when she describes her face the day she found out. Later she worked at the Westminster Hospital and in the nurses' home at St Thomas's in Ashley Gardens. One day she went to the shop to buy some cigarettes. It was closed, but she noticed that the pub next door was open. Afraid to go in herself, she asked a young man standing outside to go in for her.

'And when he come back he told me off. He said he could have run off with that pound and I would never have seen him again.' The thin, dark-haired man introduced himself as Mick Darcy. He was an Irishman, from the South, though he'd spent most of his life in London. His parents lived out in Hammersmith. He'd come home to London looking for work after being demobbed from the army after the war. Kathleen said he'd fought with Montgomery in North Africa and lost a leg in action. Mick Darcy found a job in an engineering works. He'd been on his way home from work on the evening he ran into Kathleen. The one-legged soldier and the country girl started going out together. She liked his gentleness and his sense of humour. And Mick Darcy was dependable and hard-working and he didn't drink. Coming from Kathleen's background, these were big factors in his favour.

One weekend they went down to Canvey Island, Kathleen, Mick and another couple. A few weeks later Kathleen discovered she was pregnant. Soon after this they were married. Kathleen Rolston, a Protestant from Castlederg, and Michael Darcy, a Roman Catholic from Dublin. When she told me this, the surprise must have been visible on my face. Kathleen moved away from the narrative for a few moments. 'You see, in England none of that matters. I liked England. They don't pass remarks on you over there. It doesn't matter if you marry Muhammad. You never see a clergyman from one year to another, not like this place where they're all on at you every day of the week. That was the best thing about it over there, you never thought of religion.'

And what about young Michael? I asked. Did you baptize him in a Catholic church? Kathleen said Michael had been baptized a Catholic all right. None of it mattered in England, she repeated. They settled down into a quiet family life. It was the most stable period Kathleen had ever experienced. Her father's drunkenness and violence were a long way away. So too were the hard words and swift judgements of Castlederg. London was a town you could be yourself in. Her husband was an oddball, she said, laughing. He was a loner, but he loved wee Mikey more than the world. She took out a photograph album and pointed to a small black and white picture. A tall, dark-haired man is standing with a little fair-haired boy. They are both smiling.

And then Kathleen smiled herself and remembered a story from those days. 'One Monday we took Michael to get a tooth out. You know the way they freeze your lips up? Well afterwards Mikey says to us, he says: "Mummy, they've took away my lips. They've stolen my lips." So we took him into Woolworth's and bought him a train set. Michael used to buy him all these toys. Train sets and Joe 90 and all of them. Dozens and dozens of them. Every time there was anything wrong with him he would get a toy.' She paused and said: 'They're gone now and they're not coming back.'

When Michael was four years old, his father became ill. The doctors diagnosed lung cancer and removed one lung. 'I knew for two years that he was dying. The doctors said it might be weeks, months or years, and he soldiered on for two years. Even when he was sick he went and tried to work. I used to see him going to work in the mornings but I knew well enough before two hours they would be bringing him home again. But he wouldn't ever lie in his bed. It was the world's thing to get him to lie in his bed.' One night Michael Darcy was sitting with his son, fixing a

Dinky car, when he asked Kathleen to make a cup of tea. She remembers how it looked. Big Michael on the chair and the little boy in his pyjamas at his feet. Michael Snr got up to go to the toilet. He passed Kathleen on his way out to the outhouse. 'After a while I shouted in to wee Mikey, "Did daddy come in again?" and he says, "No." And I went out and he was standing there, holding on to the bars. I went out and reached for him by the shoulder and he fell back and hit his head against the wall. He was dead.'

They buried Mick Darcy at Mortlake Cemetery. Young Michael was heartbroken. The two of them were as thick as thieves, she said. And after he'd gone young Mikey didn't know what to do. He didn't understand the business of being dead. Not for a while at any rate. Soon afterwards Kathleen had word from Castlederg that her father was sick. His relationship had ended when the woman left him for a neighbour. Now he was drinking heavily and not taking care of himself. Maybe it was fear for her father, or maybe it was the fear of being left alone and husbandless in London, but Kathleen decided to go home. She found a temporary home for herself, the little boy and the old man in an empty farmhouse outside Castlederg. But there were problems about fitting in. Her son had spent the first six years of his life in London and had a Cockney accent. How strange a world Castlederg must have seemed to him. A small country town with no traffic to speak of, no buses or great buildings and no father coming in at night to play. 'It was hard for Michael coming from England. He had a real Cockney accent although he was only six. There was a boy in this town who went by the nickname of Freddie the Frog. The other kids used to call him that. But he couldn't touch them because they all had big brothers. But Michael had no one, so Freddie used to batter him something terrible. One day I was standing at the top of the lane and young Francie came running up and said Freddie was holding Michael over the bridge with his face down into the water. By the time I got there Freddie had run off, but Michael was there crying.' Kathleen went back to her kitchen and got a knife and marched down to Freddie's house. 'I was that mad I wanted to lunge at him with the knife, only his daddy was standing there. I said to him if he ever laid a hand on Michael again I would stick the knife in his gut. And he never touched Michael again.'

But Michael's accent wasn't the only problem in Castlederg. His mother had brought him home to a very divided town. As a Protestant she naturally went to her own people for help and support. It was among Protestants that Michael would have to grow up and go to school. But his surname, Darcy, was more common in the South; it might pass as Protestant, but it might as easily be Catholic. And young Michael Darcy had been baptized a Catholic, the son of a Catholic father from the Irish Republic. 'He knew he was a Catholic. I told him,' she said. I wondered if she would have been afraid for him, if people had known about his Catholic background. 'Yeah, I would have. He wanted it quiet himself anyway 'cos he knew what they were around this place. I suppose it was the best thing to do.'

And did he remember his father? Did he ask about him?

'No. Well, he just sort of remembered him no more after we came back here. There was a time I wished we had never come back here, maybe Michael would still be alive today. But nobody knows what's going to happen, do they? My daddy died and then Michael. Then I was left on my own. Nobody.'

Kathleen had Michael rebaptized as a Protestant after they

returned to Castlederg. But the boy knew there was a Catholic half to him. And he knew it when he joined the flute band and the Ulster Defence Regiment. It was there inside him when he marched down the main street and played his Protestant tunes; it was there when he shouted taunts at the Catholic youths at the other end of the town. It was there when he got his Loyalist tattoos, there every 12th of July, every day of his life. And it was there when the IRA pumped six bullets into his back. Michael Darcy, the son of a Southern Catholic, baptized a Catholic, and none of his mates knowing. Christ, what a burden in a town like Castlederg! Was that what made him the fierce Loyalist whom Catholics detested? The fear of being neither one nor the other. The boy caught between two identities in a place that recognized no half-measures. How desperate he must have been to fit in with his English accent and his religious secret. As Kathleen told me repeatedly, Castlederg *wasn't* London. But Michael had never been found out. His mother was from a well-known Protestant family, and it didn't cross anybody's mind that she might have had a Southern Catholic husband.

By the time she was ready to tell me the story of Michael's assassination, it was late evening, and groups of teenage boys and girls were arriving at the hall across the way for band practice. Mikey had been big with the band, she said. He always gave youngsters a lift home after practice and tried to keep them out of trouble. He'd even given up his girl-friend after she asked him to choose between her and the Young Loyalists. The night he was shot he'd been at a band parade in Omagh. Kathleen always stayed awake until her son came home. At about half past twelve she heard the familiar sound of the car outside the door. 'I had a wee dog and I says to the dog "There's Mikey back", and he jumped down off the bed and ran away out. And then I heard the shots. There was six shots. I got up and ran outside. But I couldn't get the car door open. The car was locked and the engine was still running and the music was still playing and all. But I couldn't get into the car and I just stood there and screamed. And then the policeman who lived at the bottom of the road, him and his son came running. He lifted the dustbin and smashed it through the windscreen of the car, but I knew Mikey was dead. They put six bullets in his back. I could see him.'

The doctor came and Kathleen was sedated. She remembers nothing of the time leading up to the funeral. On the day it rained heavily. Michael was buried in a new plot in the graveyard on the Omagh Road. *Murdered by terrorists*, read the inscription below his name. Kathleen did not cry. She was keeping a promise made to her son at the funeral of another UDR man. *Never let them see you cry. If anything ever happens to me, never let them see you cry.* After his death came the long loneliness. Friends like Derek Hussey and her brother Herbie came to visit. Strangers like myself appeared from time to time. But Kathleen Darcy was lonely in a way that human contact or kind words could never mitigate. She remembers one night after the funeral being unable to sleep and going out to walk the roads. 'I couldn't stay in the house. I walked and walked. And then this soldier jumped out of a ditch and scared the living daylights out of me. He took me back and made me a cup of tea and put me to bed. And he stayed there all night, you know.'

Nowadays Kathleen rarely ventured out. There were trips to the hospital in Omagh, but most days she sat in watching the television. Out of the blue she started talking about the days Mikey used to take her for drives in the car. They went to Belfast and Londonderry. On Sundays in the summer they'd drive to the coast. And he took her across to Scotland three times. He'd gone to the technical school and could strip a car down to the last bolt and build it again. But there were no jobs when he left school apart from stacking shelves in Woolworth's, which he did for a while. Michael wanted to earn enough money to buy a car and so he joined up with the UDR. He got his car and then did the training to be a paramedic as well as getting a licence for driving lorries. He had planned to leave the UDR and get a job as a lorry-driver. 'He had passed the test and he was up for a job in Scotland. We were going to go to Scotland to live. But that fell through. Aye, Michael . . .' and then with her dead son's name trembling on her lips, she paused. 'He had all these plans made, but they didn't come to anything. You should never make plans.'

Kathleen and Michael. I tried to imagine them arriving off the bus on the day she returned from England when she had no plan beyond surviving. And Kathleen did her best. In hard times she took care of a dying old man and a small boy. Her boy was killed by the place he lived in, by the hatred and fear that gathered up with the centuries. Like Kathleen, I couldn't help wondering who Michael might have been had he stayed in London. Maybe he would have been one of those Londoners who switches on the news and sees Ulster and its conflict and says to himself: 'What a shower! Will they never let it go?'

Before I left Castlederg, I went back to Derek Hussey. He had been Michael's closest friend. He still visited Kathleen, drove her to the hospital and got messages for her. His name had cropped up repeatedly in her conversation. I met him back at the pub. There were few customers about and we were able to sit and chat over a drink. I didn't say anything about Michael Darcy's Catholic roots. I assumed that

Kathleen had never mentioned the fact to him. That was
something *she* could tell him if she wanted. And the truth
was, I think Derek Hussey had come far enough in his own
journey not to give a damn one way or the other. I knew
it from the many conversations we had, from the way he
talked about the peace process and his own commitment to
seeing it through.

I asked him about the night Michael was killed. What
did he remember of it all? 'We'd been at a band parade.
And afterwards we socialized together. He was very jolly,
the way he always was. He was just having a good time,
annoying nobody. I heard about the murder next morning.
A friend had arrived to do some work at my house and as
he was setting up his ladders a neighbour arrived with a
message. He was a member of the UDR and he came in
and told me. I just ran into my bedroom and cried.' But if
he was that heartbroken and angry, I wondered, how could
he even think about sitting down in the same room as Sinn
Féin?

'That is exactly why I have to think about sitting down
with them. It was Michael's death which was the catalyst
that persuaded me to enter political life. That meant sitting
in council chambers opposite Sinn Féin. I don't want there
to be any more Michael Darcys murdered like that. I want
an end to young men and women being killed.' When
Derek says this, I am listening to the voice of a man who
still mourns his dead friend. I am not listening to a politician
on the hustings. And when he tells me that it will take a
generation, maybe two, for the wounds to heal and for
people to trust one another, I believe him. He may even be
a little optimistic. But there can be healing. I used to believe
that Ulster's politicians were, by and large, a pretty hopeless
bunch. There were exceptions but not many. I was wrong

about that. There was more courage out there than I'd ever anticipated. It was there on all sides. It will be hardest out here on the margins, in places like Castlederg, far away from London and the liberal certainties of people like myself. The 11th night marches will continue and the Catholics will still resent them, seething inside their homes. But given a chance, over time, a generosity can emerge. And if some-one like Derek Hussey, in a place like Castlederg, can have the courage that he does, then perhaps Louis MacNeice was right. The son of Ulster Protestants, he wrote: 'There will be sunlight later, and the equation will come out in the end.' No certainties, of course. But no longer hoping against hope.

# 10. Quiet Conquest

It takes six hours by train from Euston. You could fly to Moscow in the same time. The journey is pretty, down through the West Country and along the Devon coast with sheer red cliffs and sparkling inlets. But when you've done it a few times in a month in midwinter, the pleasure of travel wears off; your thoughts are reduced to a numbed acceptance that Cornwall is a long, long way from the capital. There is no major airport in Cornwall, and the road journey is even longer than rail.

My friend Kevin Bishop does in fact get from London to his job in Moscow quicker than to his parents' house outside Falmouth. Kevin left Cornwall at the age of eighteen, the same year he finished school. After completing a degree in Russian, he went to work for the American television network NBC in Moscow. From there he got a job with the BBC, for whom he now ran the Moscow Bureau and occasionally travelled to the world's war zones.

We were sitting over a drink one night, after an assignment in Sierra Leone, when a discussion started up about the place each of us regarded as *home*. The third member of the group was a South African who said he liked England, but that there was only one country he would ever call his own. He 'loved' South Africa, and hardly a day went by that he didn't think about moving back. He was worried about the crime but the economy was picking up, people still had a hopeful outlook.

I said I was getting used to the idea of England being my

home; it was where I'd decided to put down roots, my child was going to school there. But if I wanted to go back to Ireland, it wouldn't be too much of a problem: with the fastest-growing economy in Europe, the country was booming.

Kevin said Cornwall was home. His parents and his brother still lived there. But he never seriously entertained thoughts of returning. Having made a name for himself in the television world, it would be surprising if he did want to go back, you might think. But the point was that unlike me or the South African, Kevin didn't really have the choice. There was no way he'd ever be able to make a viable living for himself in Cornwall, even if he wanted to. Kevin knew I was heading off on my journey around Britain in a few months' time. 'Make sure you get to Cornwall. It's like travelling to another country, honestly. People are very proud of the place, but they're seriously pissed off as well.'

I knew that Cornwall was where the Prince of Wales owned vast tracts of land; it was also where celebrities like Pete Townshend, Tim Rice and Peter de Savary had summer homes. A literary agent friend of mine had a summer home on the coast. 'The poverty isn't obvious,' he told me, 'but it's out there, believe me.' The statistics showed that Cornwall was the poorest county in England. The gross domestic product was 28.8 per cent lower than the rest of England, with unemployment 25 per cent higher than the national average. And 25 per cent is one hell of a lot of frustration, boredom and poverty.

None of this would be very obvious to the visitor, seduced by Cornwall's beauty and relieved at escaping from the coils of city life. But the county was in crisis, all right. At the last calculation, 20 per cent of the Cornish economy was derived from tourism. The traditional industries were dead or dying: the last tin mine closed at the end of the nineties, the workforce at the china clay pits around St Austell had shrunk from 6,000 to 2,500 in twenty years. The fishing industry, once a staple of the local economy, was in long-term crisis. The locals blamed the problem on the encroachments of Spanish fishing fleets (a tale familiar to Irish ears), although more detached observers blamed it on a combination of overfishing by everybody – English and Spanish together – and the inability of Cornish fishermen to compete with larger foreign vessels. And agriculture was in as great a mess in Cornwall as anywhere else in Britain.

My first port of call in Cornwall was to a dairy farm on the peninsula outside Falmouth. To reach Ben and Jackie Bailey's farm, I needed to cross the River Fal on the King Harry Ferry. The ferry was open for carrying cars and people across the river twelve hours a day from seven in the morning. On either side the banks rose up into thick woodland; it was old, mysterious country brooding over the still river. An occasional small fishing boat chugged upriver, but apart from my own car and a couple of tourists the river today was empty of traffic.

The teenager collecting money on the ferry said it was a different sight once summer began. Then people from all over England, and lots of Continentals too, would be queuing up for the ferry. I was glad I was making the journey in late autumn. On the other side I drove along a narrow wooded road; the trees were still covered with leaves, so the impression was of driving through a long rust-coloured archway. The road skirted a tidal river, a tributary of the Fal where modern yachts and old fishing boats sat temporarily marooned in the mud. Hidden behind trees and high hedges were fine summer homes, empty until warmer weather.

As I neared the coast, the countryside opened up, the

wooded hills gave way to mixed farmland: a landscape of crops – corn and kale – and herds of healthy-looking Friesians. Ben and Jackie Bailey lived here, half a mile down a narrow lane on a tenanted farm they'd been renting since 1989. The farmhouse was a small whitewashed cottage, around which patrolled two menacing geese, several ducks and chickens, and a family of guinea fowl. Set around the cottage were several barns filled with winter silage, a shed for cows that were coming close to calving time, and a smaller shed set aside for recently born animals. The Baileys lived here with their two daughters – Eloise (eight) and Alice (seventeen) – and a large black Labrador named Jude.

Ben was slightly built but gave an impression of great physical strength. He had a thin boyish face with a quick mischievous smile and a sense of humour that was tougher and drier than the Gobi Desert. But with Ben I always felt there was a lot of anger bubbling away just under the surface. He was a well-read man and sensitive about being patronized. The last thing you did with Ben Bailey was tell him you felt sorry for him. Since the farm crisis began, he'd started to become very political. He'd gone on marches with the Countryside Alliance, and, though he had little enough time for politicians as a breed, he was especially scornful of the current government.

Both he and Jackie had grown up in the town, but Ben had wanted to farm since his early boyhood. He loved the countryside and the natural world; his sitting room in the cottage was crammed with books on birds, plants, fish and animals. Jackie had settled well into the life of the farm and within ten years they had a herd of dairy cows that was among the top 10 per cent of milk producers in the country. The problem was that milk prices had collapsed in the ten years since they'd come up here to farm.

They'd started out with 77 acres and 40 cows in 1989. Seven years later they took on another 32 acres and 46 more cows. The message of the time, here as in Wales, was that you needed to be big to survive. Small farmers were going to the wall all over the country. 'I took over the farm when I was twenty-seven, and I couldn't have been more enthusiastic. I would've worked all day for nothing. I built up the herd and for six or seven years we were going along well. And then in 1996 BSE struck, and things have gone rapidly downhill.' The price he was getting for his milk had fallen by 40 per cent. And like the people who worked in manufacturing, the farmers were also suffering from the strength of the British pound.

'I've got to the stage where it's difficult to pay the bills. It's not just me, a lot of farmers out there are in difficulties. The interest charges on the money I owe are more than my profit, let alone me making any money out of it.' Ben and Jackie had run out of money. Now they owed £130,000 to the bank. The only collateral they had – just like Arwen and Gwylithin in Wales – was their livestock. They were caught between the proverbial rock and hard place. If they sold the cattle, they could give the bank something to keep them placated. The cattle cost a lot to keep; there was the feed, veterinary charges, outhouses and barns to maintain. And just now, and for the foreseeable future, there was no way the cattle were going to earn their keep. But the cattle were their only collateral. And once they were gone, what would be left to keep the bank at bay yet again?

Ben and Jackie had debated this all summer and autumn. They were proud of their dairy herd. But they had decided to sell off most of the cows. They would keep a few, and hope that the milk price improved from the sixpence a pint they were currently getting. Then they would start again and build things up as they had done in those early, hopeful days at the end of the 1980s. In the meantime they would diversify.

In practical terms this meant Ben getting a job of some kind, probably on another farm. Farmers were doing this all over the county: getting up at the crack of dawn to look after their own animals and then heading out to work on some bigger farmer's land, getting home long after dark when their children were asleep. It was what I'd seen Arwen doing back in Wales, and I knew the harm it could do to family relationships.

With Jackie the frustration and anger were there on the surface. Tears came to her eyes quickly as she talked about her family. Jackie could see the real possibility of the Bailey family losing their home. If they couldn't pay their bills and the bank moved in, they would be without a house. So most of their precious herd was going to be sold off. 'We've decided to sell the cattle because they're ours to sell. In twelve months they wouldn't be ours. At the moment they are all right, but only because we're in control. If we won the lottery on Saturday, the sale would be cancelled. We're only doing it for financial reasons. We need the money, they are our assets, and they have to go.'

The children knew this too. One evening the youngest girl, Eloise, took me out to see the calves. They were her special project: she fed them and talked to them. These calves would stay, hopefully to form the nucleus of a new herd if the situation improved. Eloise talked about the upcoming sale. She would miss the cows. Every one of them had a name, she said, and they all had different personalities. But it was the only choice her parents had. She was afraid that if they didn't sell, she and her sister wouldn't have a home to live in.

The morning of the sale, Ben took me for a walk by the coast through fields he rented from the National Trust. The air was cold, the light hard and bright. Somewhere out of sight, further down the coast, navy ships were test-firing their guns. The sound echoed through the stillness of the morning. Ben pointed to the beach below and said he went bass fishing there when he had the chance. This and shooting were his main hobbies. We shared fishing stories, and I told him I'd come and try it with him some day. He seemed unusually calm for a man who would soon have to go back to his farm and watch other farmers take away his cattle. I asked Ben if he thought his dream was dying. 'No. If I go bust, then the dream is dead. At the moment it's in intensive care. What we're trying to do is keep the dream alive.' The auctioneer had come a few days before and praised the condition of the cattle; they would fetch good prices.

Back at the farm, Jackie was out with mugs of hot tea, welcoming the men who'd come from neighbouring farms to lend a hand. She smiled and laughed and masked the anguish she was feeling inside. The auctioneers arrived and began to erect a steel ring. A mobile café sold teas and bacon sandwiches. Whenever I sought them out, Ben and Jackie were in the heart of things. Busy, busy.

I asked the auctioneers what they thought of it all. 'I don't see a future for the small farmers,' one of them said. 'A lot of people are having to sell. The whole industry is in severe crisis. Ten years ago I came up here with Ben when he started out. I couldn't have foreseen this day. I couldn't have foreseen it three years ago. But there's no indication things will get better, rather the reverse.'

The Bailey children had stayed home from school for the day. Alice was in the house helping her mother prepare food for the neighbours who'd come to support the family.

Eloise was with a friend who'd arrived to keep her company for the day. They were climbing a silage hill that was covered with plastic sheeting and tyres.

'They're hunting for toads,' said Ben, who'd come up beside me. He had changed into his overalls, ready for the sale. Cars and Land Rovers and small trucks began to arrive. Ben knew many of the people; others had come from further afield, attracted by the auctioneers' advertisement in the newspaper. When the barn had filled up, the auctioneer gave his signal to Ben. The cattle that had been lined up next door were herded one by one around the ring. There were eighty-five of them, and the sale would take several hours.

The auctioneer's voice droned over a loudspeaker: 'Through no fault of his own, this young farmer is forced to sell . . .'

Ben's expression didn't change from the moment he entered the ring until the final cow was sold. He didn't smile or grimace. He had retained the calm, distant expression I'd noticed on our cliff walk, as if he were locked away inside himself, untouched by the events taking place around him. When it was all over, his daughter Alice walked up and threw her arms around him. 'I'm proud of you,' she said. The cattle had fetched good prices. Ben would be able to pay the bank £30,000 of his £130,000 debt. Now he would start looking for a job, and in the spring things might improve.

As the new millennium dawned, the pressure grew for government action to rescue the agricultural sector. Tony Blair headed for Cornwall to listen to farmers' complaints. He met one farmer whose accounts showed he was earning 33 pence an hour. The government responded with a £200 million rescue package. It was good news, but in the long term the effect was bound to be limited. Much of the sympathy one heard from government ministers had a feel of 'duty' about it, as if the government had quietly come to the same conclusion as each of its predecessors: why exert a major effort to rescue an industry that represents just 2 per cent of the labour force, and whose long-term decline seems inexorable? It seemed that the truly compelling arguments about community were lost in the general antagonism of the debate.

The farmers' problems were only one part of the crisis of rural Britain. In Cornwall, as indeed in vast areas of Wales, the Midlands and the north of England, there were growing social problems that mirrored the crisis of the big city estates. West Country towns like Yeovil were reporting frightening increases in the level of drug abuse; a police report in Norwich disclosed that six addicts had died in a period of one week in April 1998; Class A drugs were now as easy to come by in Taunton as they were in Toxteth. None of this was evolving in a dramatic, headline-grabbing way. You followed this story by reading the court cases in the local newspapers and by ferreting through the detail of official reports.

Or you could spend a few days in the company of a woman like Hazel Stuteley. Hazel was a health visitor in Falmouth and had spent a decade working on the town's Beacon Estate. Fair-haired and petite, Hazel was fifty-one years old and had been a nurse all her working life. She had grown up in a rural community in Hampshire and gone to London for nursing training. 'I was useless at school, I was too interested in the Beatles and all that to study, but I did like working with what you might call disadvantaged people. It started out as summer work helping kids with learning disabilities, and then I came to London to King's College Hospital to train in nursing.' She qualified in 1968 and one day asked a health visitor if she could come with her on a trip to Deptford. The experience was to shape her life. 'We went to this one house and I'll never forget it, the state of the place. There was a woman the same age as me but who looked much, much older. Her teeth were going, her skin looked terrible, and she had these five kids running around this filthy, falling-down flat. And I looked up and saw on the mantelpiece a picture of her on her wedding day. She was all done up in her wedding dress and smiling, a totally different person. I said to myself: "What happened to her, what turned her into the person I saw before me? Why didn't somebody help her?"'

The Deptford visit was the catalyst. But after I'd learned a lot more about Hazel and her family, it wasn't too hard to see that idealism was also part of her heritage. Her father, Charles Edward Honeysett, was the son of a carpenter from Hailsham in East Sussex. The family were poor, and at the age of thirteen he left school and worked as a clerk around the county, before joining the army on his eighteenth birthday. He was just in time to be sent to France to face the great German counter-attack along the Western Front in 1917. In Flanders he fought with the Royal Irish Fusiliers as Haig's army was driven back by massive German bombardments. Charles Honeysett remembered the terror of having to dig a foxhole with his bare hands. His diary records that 125 men died in half an hour.

He survived, and came home a convinced believer in the rights of small nations. Throughout the thirties he involved himself in campaigns against fascism, speaking at Hyde Park Corner to indifferent passers-by, and eventually being called to arms again to fight Hitler. Because of his age the War

Office made him a clerk and in that role he accompanied Churchill's delegation to the Quebec Conference with Roosevelt. After the war, he came home to his wife and they started a family. Their daughter Hazel was born in 1949.

The house of her childhood was a profoundly political place. The ideals Hazel's father had carried with him from war to peace – social justice, resistance to oppression – were handed on to his children.

They were certainly a big part of the reason why Hazel chose to be a health visitor in the NHS. At the start she worked in inner London, and then in 1975 she and her husband and their two young sons moved down to Cornwall. Her third son was born in the county. They moved to get away from the city, in search of the rural idyll that Cornwall seemed to promise. Hazel found a job as a health visitor and found the idyll was nothing of the sort. 'There was a beautiful frame here but a very depressing picture. Not that you'll see it if you come through on your holidays. It's hidden poverty and the people are proud. You won't see them begging or shouting about their poverty, but it's here, all right.'

It isn't just the tourists who don't see the reality. Hazel spends a lot of her time giving talks to local business people. 'I went into the Rotary Club here in Falmouth to tell them what it was like for people living on the Beacon Estate, the kind of problems they face, and they had no idea. There were people who said they never even knew the estate existed. And why would they? Why would people make a point of finding out? From the outside it just looks like lots of council houses on a hill. But behind those walls are so many stories.'

Coming to the end of this British journey, I had a fair

idea of the kind of stories Hazel was talking about. Violence, drugs, intimidation of neighbours. The Beacon Estate was built on a hill overlooking Falmouth Harbour. It sat directly above the town's yachting marina; the expensive boats and apartments could be seen from the windows of the estate houses. The Beacon had started life after the war to provide modern housing for poor families. The poor were moved from one part of town to another. But they were still poor and crammed together into an estate of poor housing, houses that managed to be both cramped and cold. There were 6,000 people living in 1,500 houses on the Beacon, and 80 per cent of them were receiving some form of benefit.

You could tell that Hazel was trusted and liked. People stopped in the street to ask her questions or chat. And if a child was in trouble somewhere or something was going seriously wrong with a family, she was one of the few people in the whole structure of officialdom that the residents would trust enough to talk to.

The first house we visited was occupied by a mother and her eighteen-year-old daughter. The father was 'away' and the son was in prison. I will call the woman 'Tanya'. The two women were watching television in the sitting room when we came in. Another girl joined us and said her name was 'Joanne' and that she was a friend of Tanya's daughter. Joanne had been thrown out of her home a few days before. She was sixteen and said her mother had a new boyfriend who wanted her out of the place. Before she left, her mother had packed her clothes and then urinated on them.

Tanya's daughter was listening to all of this and watching my and Hazel's expressions with a sly smile. She sat on the couch with her legs folded underneath her. When Joanne had finished telling her story, her friend spoke. 'I'd have fucking done her if she'd done that to me. I wouldn't have let her get away with it.' Joanne said nothing. I imagined her mother and the new boyfriend were a pretty tough combination.

Tanya's daughter was eighteen and pregnant. She told Hazel that since becoming pregnant she'd given up drugs. The girl had been arrested 150 times and been 'inside' seven times. Most of her arrests were for shoplifting and fighting. She stole to pay for her drugs habit. On the Beacon, speed was the drug of choice. I asked how she'd got into drugs in the first place. She said the dealers came up to the kids and gave them 'lay-ons', free samples to entice them into developing a habit. And for a lot of the bored, unemployed kids from screwed-up families, this must indeed have seemed like an act of generosity: a free high to carry them up and away from their hemmed-in lives. The drug dealers were all over the place, she said. Then Joanne explained that her boyfriend had been a dealer. She split up with him because he was violent, but not before she got sent to prison for storing his drugs.

Tanya herself was going crazy because of trouble with a neighbouring family. They were notorious criminals and had been threatening her kids. It would have been impossible there and then to have established the rights and wrongs of the row, but Tanya was certainly very scared. The family had been up to her house several times looking for a fight in the past few days. Tanya wanted out of the Beacon, but didn't think there was much chance of getting anywhere nicer. Her main hope now was that the council would respond to pressure from other harassed residents and move her dangerous neighbours.

We said goodbye and walked along the street towards the next family. On estates like the Beacon, families tended to fall into four categories: there were the ones who struggled on against the odds, who worked in lousy, low-paid jobs or struggled by on benefit and tried to keep their children safe and happy; there were the ones who had problems with alcohol, drugs and money but who didn't generally bother their neighbours; then came the families who had all the social vices and who took pleasure in bothering their neighbours, the dangerous brigade that people warned their children to avoid; and there was a fourth, a more secret and quiet category, the 'strange' families for whom people felt pity and whom they avoided like the plague.

It was in this category that 'Janice' and 'Mark' and their five children languished. Before going in, Hazel warned me to expect a mess. 'The kids here are on the "at risk" register,' she said. 'I can't tell you why, but maybe Janice will if you get talking to her.' Hazel knocked on the door and it was opened by a small, heavy-set woman with dark hair and a worried-looking expression. When Janice saw that her caller was Hazel, she smiled. Immediately we were surrounded by several small children. They swarmed around Hazel, pushing each other to get close to her. Janice threw her eyes up to heaven and beckoned to us to come in. The hallway opened directly into a kitchen that was overcrowded and dirty. There were dirty dishes and clothes scattered everywhere along with fragments of bicycles and toys, and in the middle of it all hung a strip of flypaper, thick with dead insects. I could hear the sound of birdsong coming from the sitting room. I looked in and saw that an aviary had been built into the alcove next to the fire. Several budgies flew back and forth, rustling and whistling behind the wire. The room was crammed with bric-à-brac. There were more toys and old suitcases; a stereo and a television, and above the mantelpiece a display of photographs. One was of an old man in a seaman's uniform. Mark explained that this was his dad, who'd fished and worked on boats around Falmouth before the fishing went bad. Most of the photographs were of the children: there were eleven-year-old twins, a boy and a girl, a nine-year-old girl, a seven-year-old boy and a six-month-old baby boy.

Neither Mark nor Janice had a job. Mark had hurt his back in an industrial accident five years before and was suing for compensation. He was a sad and meek-looking man. He was gentle around the children, and they seemed to gravitate naturally towards him. Janice came across as tough and defensive, although she clearly liked Hazel. I learned later that Janice's relationship with social workers was famously bad. Hazel produced her weighing scales and the children lined up to be weighed. Unhappy or abused children tended to lose weight, she said. Hazel kept a daily eye on families like this, making sure that whatever was happening in the adults' lives, the kids didn't go hungry.

You couldn't tell from first glance that these children were troubled. They ran around the house, playing with and teasing each other like normal. Just boisterous children, you would think, trapped in too small a space. But they were cautious around their mother. And when the little boy asked if he could go out and play, she deliberately ignored him. He asked again, and she continued to ignore him. After a third attempt, she looked at him and shook her head. He left the room and went upstairs without saying a word.

A few days later I went back on my own. Janice and Mark were there, the children were out at school. The couple were happy to talk about life on the estate and what was happening with their kids. Janice volunteered the information that they were on the 'at risk' register. 'I have this bad temper, so I'm not allowed to hit 'em. I can't hit 'em. So I don't lose me temper now.'

I asked if anything in particular had happened that had led to social services becoming involved.

'I tried to kill me daughter,' she said. 'I got mad with her and got me hands round her throat and was choking her.'

That was as much of the story as she wanted to tell. But I asked around and learned some more. The eldest boy had taken to starting fires and had been running away from home and school. The nine-year-old girl was a chronic bed-wetter. And the little boy – the one I'd seen abruptly dismissed from Janice's presence – had been getting into trouble at school for disrupting the class. It didn't require genius to figure out something was seriously wrong here.

'What do you think of all that?' I asked her, after our last visit.

'It breaks my heart. It really does,' she said. And though nothing on earth gave me the right to make any assumptions about these children, I couldn't help feeling that the point of rescue had long passed. Maybe with the smaller boy and the baby there was some chance. But the others? Down here at the end of England, in the last days of this journey, I could not find it in myself to feel anything but despair.

And that was where the story might have ended, if someone like Hazel Stuteley wasn't around to point out the other journey. She didn't come out with glib lines about seeing the bright side, or try to convince me that wonderful government initiatives were going to transform life. There was no vacuous official speak about the need to be 'positive'. But the people of the Beacon had begun a journey of their own. Five years ago Hazel and her colleague Phillip Trenowith suggested that the people set up their own resi-dents' committee. At the time there were many in the local establishment – she won't say who – who advised them to ignore the residents. 'They don't want to change,' she was told. But Hazel and Phillip persevered. And on a bitterly cold December night in 1995 they called the first ever meeting of the Beacon Residents' Association. Only six people turned up, but it was enough to get things started.

The meetings started to attract more support. Then the residents set up a partnership with the police and local council, and applied for funding to regenerate the estate. The building stock was so bad that some houses were scoring zero on the SAP register that monitors the condition of local authority housing. It takes a lot of damp or subsidence or structural damage to score as low as zero. In total the residents had won grants of £2.2 million to revive the estate. There were 1,500 houses and two thirds would benefit from the regeneration. The Association campaigned for the introduction of traffic-calming measures. The council stonewalled them. So they went and produced their own detailed report; when it landed in front of the council, the officials were convinced an expensive firm of consultants had been employed to prepare it. Traffic calming was introduced. A mother and baby group was set up and a group for young mothers suffering from post-natal depression. In two years the rate of post-natal depression fell by 80 per cent. Since 1995 house burglaries were down by over 40 per cent, assault was down by 60 per cent – the overall crime rate was half what it was when the Association started out. There was a marked improvement on the education front too: the pass rate for boys sitting SATS had improved by 100 per cent. And the headmaster of a local primary school was pleased to announce that parents no longer beat each other up outside the school gates.

It was small news on a national scale. But in a place like

the Beacon – written off, abandoned – it was a phenomenal achievement. And the Residents' Association is still going strong; the next project will be a new play area for the children. When you asked residents why the Association worked, they invariably said it was because the people running it didn't talk down to them. The Association belonged to them, it spoke their language. No less a figure than Tony Blair presented Hazel and Phillip with the NHS Nye Bevan 1999 award for the Beacon community's achievements.

While I was writing this chapter, Hazel's brother Jon sent me a poem written by their father after he'd survived the battle of Mount Kemmel in Flanders. He wrote it while watching the swaying of a bluebell that had somehow survived the German bombardment. The poem is called 'Quiet Conquest'. It was written in the aftermath of battle, with the smell of dead bodies still heavy in the air. It is not a conventional poetic masterpiece; if you did not know the context in which it had been written, it might seem trite and sentimental. But the magic of this poem is that such spirit of warmth could have survived the horror of the battle. I quote the poem for all the people I met along the road, for the abandoned and abused and those who fight on their behalf.

> A bluebell stood on Kemmel Hill;
> it bowed and smiled as bluebells will.
> The cheeky thing – it didn't care,
> though shells begrudged its presence there.
> The tortured earth was gouged and rent
> by reeking shells on murder bent –
> the bluebell stood on Kemmel Hill,
> dispensing nature's magic still.

Perhaps it isn't something that
anyone should wonder at;
when wickedness would evil do,
virtue doesn't want it to.
So make a stand and hold your ground,
that purity and grace abound,
truth asserts her sovereign will,
and bluebells grow on Kemmel Hill.

– Pte Martin Honeysett, Flanders, 1917

# Epilogue
## People Like Us

I am sitting in my study in west London, surrounded by a small mountain of notebooks, audio cassettes, reference books, official reports and letters. Most of the letters are from people I met along the road. Letters from Glasgow, north Wales, Leeds, Cornwall.

In Govan, where I started out on my journey, Jamie Webster and the men are waiting to hear if the Ministry of Defence will grant the yard a contract to build new roll-on/roll-off ferries. At the time of writing the omens are not good. The speculation is that the contract will go to a German yard. Jamie's men have enough work on the books to keep the yard open for another eighteen months . . . and then? Nobody wants to say the word, but closure could be looming again.

Outside the gates Davy McCuish is still searching for a job, and Geraldine McCaskell in Money Matters is still patiently sorting through the tangled lives of the debt-ridden. But she hasn't seen or heard from Marie, the single mother who has vanished with her two young boys. They are out there somewhere, but Geraldine doesn't have the time or resources to search for them.

In Leeds Fiona Stewart, the heroin addict whose boy-friend died from an overdose, had disappeared as well. When I say 'disappeared', I mean she had gone somewhere that I or the police would never find her. I kept thinking about the warning the hospital had given her: 'If you keep using, you will die.' And then, literally as this book was going to press, she called me on my mobile. Fiona sounded bright and cheerful. She'd been in hospital again, she said. Another blood clot and more dire warnings from the hospital staff. But for the past two months she hadn't had any heroin. She had been prescribed the heroin substitute methadone and was getting her life back together. Who knows how Fiona will fare in the future. But she is trying.

Lucy Collinson, the old woman who'd been attacked for her pension, is living in an old people's home in Leeds and will never return to her flat on Lincoln Green. Her relatives say she has never recovered from the mugging.

Back on the estate Louise, the young mother who wanted her children to get an education and escape the poverty trap, is still sitting down patiently every night and going through their homework. She is making small steps on a very long road, but I believe the family will reach the place it needs to be.

From Wales I received a letter from Gwylithin as the lambing season approached. Twenty-two lambs had already arrived. 'Soon I'll be pulling a lamb out and feeding the five thousand the next . . . men get it so easy,' she wrote. 'They come in, food on the table – no washing up, but we have to help outside, prepare the food, look after the children, make the fire, run to the vets . . . the list goes on! I wish I was cloned!'

The letter was mostly full of local news. There was an *eisteddfod* at the chapel and her gran had been taken ill in the middle of the performance. It was nothing too serious, gallstones that would be removed in an operation later in the year. At the end she added a postscript: 'While making the accounts out, I discovered that during Dec., Jan. and Feb. we were at a loss of £7,647. That's why this life depresses me now.'

   Down in Cornwall, Hazel and the tenants on the Beacon Estate are planning other ways to regenerate the area; at the top of their list is a project to create more playing space for the children. Whenever I called her, Hazel bubbled with enthusiasm. And she never tired of reminding me: 'You can't just sit around moaning. You've got to do something.'

   In London I've stayed in touch with the pensioner Ron Roberts, calling up to see him whenever I get the chance. He is struggling badly with his eyesight and ventures out very rarely. His tiny garden on the balcony is still untended. But he says that next spring he will get round to planting again.

   In Ulster things are looking bleak for supporters of the Good Friday Agreement. The hardliners in the Unionist camp have pulled the party further away from political reality, refusing to rejoin negotiations unless the Royal Ulster Constabulary is allowed to retain its name. Even Derek Hussey finds himself pulled in the direction of the hard liners. He wants arms decommissioning before he will sit down again with Sinn Féin. Although a return to full-scale violence looks unlikely, the prospects for a healing of the bitter wounds in places like Castlederg are hardly propitious. More likely, the old siege will continue until the reality of having to co-exist and make a future together impinges once again on the leaders of both traditions.

   As I travelled along the British margins, I heard people repeatedly begin sentences with the phrase 'people like us'. It was used always to describe a condition of exclusion. *People like us haven't the money to buy a house; people like us have no choice about where we send our kids to school; people like us have to live with junkies next door.* Nowhere did I find an atmosphere of outright despair. What did exist was a kind of exhausted anger, anaesthetized for many by alcohol and drugs and the tranquillizing tedium of television.

The drug crisis defied any expectation I might have had. Crack and heroin are *everywhere* in the undercountry. While hip Britain parties with cocaine and counts its money, the children of the poor beg, steal and sell their bodies to get a fix. Some of them die from it and lots of them go to jail. As I was writing this book, a report appeared calling for the legalization of soft drugs like cannabis. The media broadly support the idea. The world and its mother know the police are losing the battle. Why not free them up to go after the really big drug lords? Fair enough, you might say. But nowhere in the debate did anybody wonder why our instinctual response is to believe you could solve a problem like this by banning or by liberalizing. The idea that we might begin to tackle the profoundly addictive culture of our society appears far too challenging a proposition. People are addicted to crack, heroin, alcohol and the rest because they want to escape. They won't stop being addicted if you legalize the stuff. Nor will people who have no money suddenly stop robbing and mugging to feed their habits. The current debate is about law enforcement, not about the causes and cures for the social and personal tragedy of addiction. The 'cure' will be a long hard road; it will involve jobs and housing, and getting addiction counsellors on to the big estates, and it will involve a fundamental change in the values of society.

You pick up your newspaper and read that a three-month-old baby has swallowed heroin left lying around by his parents; two little boys are killed by their parents in a squalid council flat; a child is left wearing a plaster cast for ten months by its addict mother; an eighteen-year-old schizophrenic girl is murdered for fun by children her own age; 69-year-old John Sheppard's body is found in his flat in Brent *three and a half years* after he is believed to have died. You read all of this and you still won't know a fraction of what is happening out there. This is just the abuse and abandonment that reaches some kind of conclusion in the courts or in death. Most of what goes on is hidden from the public gaze.

The Prime Minister promises that child poverty will be eradicated by the year 2020. It is a noble goal. But even in the time that he has set, how many lives will be destroyed, how much unhappiness handed down to the next generation? The family, which politicians like to describe as the cornerstone of society, has never faced greater pressure. There are the obvious threats of poverty and addiction and abuse. These are tangible and can be targeted by specific action, if there is the political will. But more insidious is the obsession with the material that pervades our entire society and piles pressure on the poor to buy what they cannot afford. Children mock and bully other children because of the clothes they wear, a peer group pressure that sends kids home every day with a new demand. Poverty is more than a condition of not having; it is the humiliating scramble to keep up with the demands of a society that defines worth in terms of wealth. Perhaps we should consider how it might feel to be permanently excluded from this 'golden circle'.

The country through which I travelled was a place of profound divisions. I am aware that that is a very overt statement of the obvious. *So tell us something new.* The figures – widely published – are shocking: a trebling of child poverty in twenty years; 18 per cent of males under the age of twenty-five unemployed; farm incomes falling from an average of £18,000 to £4,500 in a single year.

But it is not as simple as counting the numbers of those who have wealth and those who have very little or none. The facts tell us only part of the story. Nor does the stereotypical notion of a north/south divide in any way reflect the reality of life on the British margins. The crisis is not a geographical one: poverty and alienation exist throughout Britain. Often the people of the margins live cheek by jowl with conspicuous wealth, as in the cases of Lincoln Green in Leeds or the Beacon Estate in Cornwall. The greater separation is in the reality of daily experience and expectation. The man on Lincoln Green who lives without a job, whose neighbours are drug addicts or alcoholics, is as foreign to my middle-class world as a Bosnian or a Somali. He is a citizen of another country, an *undercountry* where the horizon hits you smack in the face the moment you walk out of the flat. Likewise, the tenant farmers whose way of life is vanishing feel themselves to be profoundly at odds with the new Britain.

But unlike for the refugee from another country, there was no possibility of foreign sanctuary for the excluded citizens of Britain. They stayed where they were because they had no choice. Some of the struggling farmers in Scotland did abandon their land and head for Canada. But they were a small group. Most of the tenant farmers stayed in Britain, part of the country but excluded from its general prosperity.

If the unemployed man living on a sink estate watched the news or read the papers he would know that politicians and commentators referred to him as socially excluded. There is another word for their condition: *invisible*. It is not that the establishment has failed to see the need for social change, or that there has been a lack of will for reform. The problem is that most politicians and commentators haven't the remotest notion of what it is like to live without power and without choice.

Short of insisting that the political and media élite spend a mandatory period living in a tower block or tramping the Welsh hills in cold weather, how is it possible to address this crisis of difference? Perhaps a large part of the answer lies in going into communities and learning the truth of people's daily experience. The political culture in Britain remains deeply paternalistic. There is a functioning democracy in the sense that people have a vote and they have political organizations that can represent their views. There is a free press through which society can express the plurality of difference. But it is essentially a 'top down' model of democracy. There are town and borough councils but they are hugely bureaucratic instruments, not the kind of places where the poor or excluded can feel sure of having their voices heard.

One of the most effective means of ensuring that people do not feel voiceless is to promote a vigorous civil society. I know from my experience in apartheid South Africa that this was one of the most important factors in defusing the anger that could all too easily have erupted into civil war. Though people were denied a vote, they still had groups and forums through which they could express their feelings and effect some change, however modest, in their environment. There is no lack of willing individuals in Britain. In places as far apart as Glasgow, Leeds and Cornwall, I encountered vibrant civic groups dedicated to effecting change. They had pathetically limited resources, but they were passionate about their communities.

None of what they do – campaigning for playgrounds,

running mother and baby groups, taking children to the seaside – captures the national headlines. But it is making a difference. As Kath Barber kept reminding me in Leeds, it is about *ownership* and *belonging*. Whether it is the children who turn up every day at the Lincoln Green Youth Base or Hazel Stuteley's tenants fighting to regenerate the Beacon Estate in Cornwall, there is an unmistakable sense of pride in belonging. It exists throughout marginal Britain, this longing for community; the cult of selfish individualism has not yet won out.

The 'big picture' of government policy will hopefully effect meaningful change in the lives of the excluded. There has been a change in the political atmosphere; the concept of social exclusion as a real and pressing crisis is now almost universally accepted and the will for major change does exist. But it is at ground level that we need to invest. It will take money and attention, not speeches or think-tanks – and listening to what people have to say, making the funds available to transform the estates into fit places to raise families. So often it is what appears to be the small thing that is needed: the funding for a crèche or an elderly daycare centre can make the biggest difference to the everyday living experience. In eighteen months of travelling I continually met people who knew exactly what was wrong with their communities, and who had sensible things to say about what could be done. The scale of the problems is so vast – drugs in particular – that it is tempting to believe we won't be able to turn the tide. But that is wrong. Real change is possible. It is a job that will take twenty to thirty years, maybe longer, but its effects will transform the lives of generations. This is still a country of heroes. The problem is that we all too rarely choose to see them. They are out there in the most unlikely places. I met them in Govan and

Leeds, in the hills of north Wales, by the coast in Falmouth, on the County Tyrone border and in the heart of London. Forget the politicians who promise to put the 'Great' back into Britain. It is already there, right before our eyes.

# Select Bibliography

Borrow, George, *Wild Wales: Its People, Language and Scenery* (London, first pub. 1862; 1998 ed.)

Centre for Policy on Ageing (CPA), *The Social Policy of Old Age* (London, 1999)

*The Complete Handbook to Life in Leeds*, ed. Mark Young (Leeds, 1998)

Donnelly, Patrick, *Govan on the Clyde* (Glasgow, 1994)

Faley, Jean, *Up Oor Close: Memories of Domestic Life in Glasgow Tenements 1910–1945* (Oxford, 1990)

Foster, R. F., *Modern Ireland 1600–1972* (London, 1988)

Gilbert, Martin, *A History of the Twentieth Century. Volume 1: 1900–1933* (London, 1997)

Heaney, Seamus, *Selected Poems 1965–1975* (London, 1980)

Help the Aged reports

    MORI/Help the Aged, *Home Truths: A Survey of People Aged Sixty-five and Over* (London, May 1996)

    Tessa Harding, *A Life Worth Living: The Independence and Inclusion of Older People* (London, 1997)

    Help the Aged/Centre for Policy on Ageing, *Living Alone and Dying Alone* (joint seminar proceedings, London, April 1999)

McKittrick, David, Kelters, Seamus, Feeney, Brian, and Thornton, Chris, *Lost Lives: The Stories of Men, Women and Children Who Died as a Result of the Northern Ireland Troubles* (Edinburgh, 1999)

Morgan, Kenneth O., *The People's Peace: British History since 1945* (Oxford, 1990)

Moss, Michael, *The Clyde: A Portrait of a River* (Edinburgh, 1996)

*Mungo's City: A Glasgow Anthology*, eds. Brian D. Osborne and Ronald Armstrong (Edinburgh, 1999)

The Scottish Council Foundation, *Three Nations: Social Exclusion in Scotland* (Edinburgh, 1998)

Skidmore, Ian, *A Gwynedd Anthology* (Swansea, 1992)

# Acknowledgements

This is above all a book of human stories. To find these stories I entered the lives of families all over Britain. It is to them that I owe the greatest debt of gratitude. They opened their homes and their hearts, they willingly went back into the history of their families and the areas in which they lived. For many it required singular courage to sit for hours with a stranger and describe the past and present of their lives. It would be wrong to single out individuals; suffice to say that their generosity and openness will be remembered by me as long as I live.

There were many people involved with local community organizations, voluntary groups or statutory bodies who gave freely of their time and advice. Among those whose cooperation was invaluable were: Kath Barber and Sue Balcombe in Lincoln Green, Leeds; Hazel Stuteley and Philip Trenowith of the Falmouth Health Centre; Geraldine McCaskill of Money Matters in Glasgow; Assemblyman Derek Hussey in Castlederg; the Information Department of Islington Council; Tessa Harding, Daniel Pearson and Hilary Carter at Help the Aged in London; Reg Heaydon of the Tenant Farmers Association and Nan Owen of Cerri-gydrudion Primary School, Wales.

At the BBC my thanks to director James Hayes for suggesting the idea of a journey in the first place. He was assisted by a wonderful team of producers: Nicola Gibson, Sue Belton, Rachel Crellin and Julie Dark. Alex Hanson and Tim Day were always a pleasure to work with as was

Jane Wright, the empress of logistics. Manisha Vadhia of the Political Documentaries Unit is owed a particular debt of gratitude for her work in Ulster. My thanks also to Peter Salmon, Controller of BBC 1, to Paul Hamman at BBC Documentaries and to Richard Sambrook and Adrian Van Klaveren at BBC News.

At Penguin Books my publisher Tony Lacey was patient beyond words as deadlines slipped and slipped. Having dealt with me now for nearly eight years he knows precisely when and how to apply the pressure. It is always deceptively gentle, and the book *always* gets written. Editor Donna Poppy has also laboured over my late manuscripts before; she is a punctilious editor and a merciless enemy of the careless phrase. Thanks as well to Charlotte Greig at Penguin publicity who has struggled with ever changing deadlines.

My agent David Godwin has been a determined presence and his comments on the text were invaluable. He is endlessly attentive. Others whose views were highly valued were Timothy Sheehy in Oxford, Chris Wyld and Mike O'Driscoll in London, Colin Blane in Brussels and 'Jacob', my point of contact with the drug-using community in Leeds. Kevin Bishop, a Cornishman trapped in Moscow, offered a valuable perspective on his native county. John Lynch and Mary McGuckian offered discerning feedback on the Ulster chapters. Thanks as well to my close friends Johnny, Gordon and Errol for the friendship and moral support which helped sustain me throughout the past year. They were a constant source of challenge and laughter. My most profound debt of gratitude goes to my wife Anne and son Daniel. Anne was as ever a wise critic as well as having taken on the task of researching the statistical data used in the book. Though this was not a journey into a life-

threatening war zone, it did involve me spending consider-
able time away from home. The forbearance shown by my
family is hugely appreciated.